INCLINED TOWARD MAGIC

Also by David Meyer

Memoirs of a Book Snake:
Forty Years of Seeking and Saving Old Books

Inclined toward MAGIC

DAVID MEYER

WALTHAM STREET PRESS

See the Credits section beginning on page 163,

LIBRARY OF CONGRESS CATALOGING-IN-PUBLICATION DATA

Meyer, David, 1943–
Inclined toward magic : encounters with books, collectors
and conjurors / David Meyer.
p. cm.
Includes index.
ISBN 0-916638-55-3
1. Meyer, David, 1943– 2. Book collectors—United States—
Biography. 3. Book collecting—United States—Anecdotes.
4. Magic—Collectibles—United States. 5. Magicians—
United States—Anecdotes. 6. Magic—Bibliography. I. Title.
Z989.M49M49 2003
002'.075—dc21

2003045013

Waltham Street Press is an imprint of
Meyerbooks, *Publisher*
P.O. Box 427, Glenwood, IL 60425

for

JAY MARSHALL

Magician
Vaudevillian
Ventriloquist
Puppeteer
Punch-and-Judy Man
Comedian
Shadowgraphist
Troublewit Artist
Limerick Writer
Magic Historian
Editor
Publisher
Book Collector
Friend

Nostalgia's here. I see in every room
Our own eyes mirrored, our heads turn, our tricks,
Our ways. I hear our words.

JEAN PARRISH

Contents

Illustrations

Thanks to

Mary Parrish for her careful editing
and helpful suggestions

Jim Alfredson, whose knowledge of magic
far exceeds mine, for reading the manuscript
and offering valuable advice

My wife, Anita, for her endless
encouragement and support in all things

And a pat on the head of our loyal dachshund, Margo,
who often sat impatiently at my feet as I worked,
wanting me to do something else

A NOTE TO THE READER

THIS IS MY SECOND VOLUME of book tales. The contents of the first, *Memoirs of a Book Snake: Forty Years of Seeking and Saving Old Books,* are fairly described in the title. The misnomer "snake" instead of book*worm* came about through a malapropism uttered by my friend Frances Marshall (1910–2002). She and her husband, Jay, figure prominently in the present volume and it seems wise to introduce them here, at the beginning. Frances was a magic dealer, performer, writer and mentor to many in magic and Jay is everything I have listed in this book's dedication—and more.

Many of the readers who wrote me about *Book Snake* expressed a wish that it could have been longer. The easy answer would be: If I had found more books and had more interesting experiences, it would have been. But the truth is, for half of my forty years as a book collector I was deeply involved in the pursuit of books on magic, and the subject did not fit comfortably in the first volume. That's the reason for the second.

There will not be a third. I have written all I care to on the subject of books and collecting. Other memories pull at me now.

Introduction

THE SO-CALLED WORLD OF MAGIC—not including the occult variety—is a microcosm of talented performers, inventors and innovators. They are admired by a legion of ardent amateurs whose interest is sustained by magic shops, clubs, magazines, books and videos. Among the members of this group are a noticeable number of egoists and oddballs. I fall into the second category. I have not performed magic since my boyhood. Nor do I hanker to learn the secret of the newest illusion or pocket trick. In my youth I routinely purchased the latest mystery on the market and added it to a stash of others. This practice continues to fill a lot of my fellow enthusiasts' dens and closets, but I long ago gave it up. Yet I am so much in love with books on the subject—both those explaining how to perform magic and those chronicling the histories of great conjurors—that not only have I been a collector for over forty years, I became a publisher of such books myself. This book, likely to be one of the oddest of my output, concerns what I've been up to in the world of magic without being a magician.

How did I find my way into this sideline of my life? My first magic book was a copy of Albert Hopkins' *Magic Stage Illusions and Scientific Diversions including Trick Photography*, published in 1897 by Scientific American and purchased for me by my father in the rare book department of Marshall Field's department store in the 1950s. I think now that my father bought it reluctantly, for it was hardly a practical book for a ten-year-old would-be magician and its price, ten dollars, was more than he was paying for books he bought for himself. But it might have charmed him almost as much as it did me. Its 400 illustrations of stage mechanics and apparatus trickery, black art and optical illusions forever anchored my affections in the romantic realm of Victorian magic. Perhaps that's one of the reasons I never became an accomplished magician: my ambitions belonged to the 19th century with its nickeled props and hidden trap doors in a stage floor. I found the book far more fascinating than most others and I turn to it still, five decades after acquiring it.

The second magic book I acquired was also my first mistake as a book collector. I found it in a dim and dusty shop on Wabash Avenue in Chicago. This street lies beneath the shadows of elevated train tracks. The shop—now long gone and its name forgotten—held an indefinable attraction when, in fact, it was little more than a junk shop. Unlike the carefully displayed books in Field's antiquarian department, in this place most of the books were heaped in piles on the floor and counters. Some, however, were displayed within a glass-fronted bookcase, where they appeared more precious and important than they were. How else can I explain why I became enchanted with a copy of Joseph Ovette's pamphlet *Magician's New Field*? Not only was this book unattractive, it was in a condition that cried out, "Leave me be!" Surely this poor copy must have been carried by a serviceman through every campaign of World War II. It had been crudely rebound within olive-drab canvas covers, the same material used to make duffel bags. Its original cover was pasted roughly over the canvas, and for the final defacement, a three-hole punch had taken its toll on the inside margins of the text. Why would I ever *want* such a book?

Part of the reason was my inexperience. I was shopping with my grandmother rather than my father on this occasion and this difference was crucial. Instead of having the counsel of a book buyer with experience, I had access to an open purse. But another, more common reason better explains it: I was hunting magic books and this was the only one in the store.

I bought it (or rather my grandmother Grace did, for she was the one with the purse), but afterwards I never felt comfortable having or even holding the book. For years I kept it hidden behind others in my bookcase. Every time I saw it I was sorry I had ever bought it; yet I kept it for the simple, sentimental reason that it was one of the first magic books I had owned. Having rescued it from the junk shop and given it a good home, I found it impossible to cast it away. As my collection grew, *Magician's New Field* was pushed around and out into the open again and again, until it eventually migrated to the basement where it joined accumulations of other unwanted books. Finally, when I began selling magic books in addition to buying them, I found a reason to get rid of it, and someone actually purchased it. My one remaining concern regarding this sad copy was that someday it might somehow turn up again in a book collection I would buy.

I first became aware of the term "magic book collector" when I bought a copy of *The Life and Times of Augustus Rapp, The Small Town Showman.* This delightful volume was published in 1959 by Jay Marshall for the Ireland Magic Company, the business operated by his wife, Frances. Magician and author Robert Parrish wrote the introduction, and the scene he set for Rapp's account of life "on the road" is a classic in itself. Jay's preface explained how the original manuscript was retyped on "an old typewriter" after the typist was given "five minutes of verbal instructions." The completed text was then reproduced (typos, smudges and all) and interspersed with old photographs, playbills and anything else Jay could find (or illustrate himself when necessary), capturing in print the homespun charm which Rapp's narrative conveys.

The edition was spiral bound with plastic covers, and the binder added tissue paper "guards" to keep the covers unscratched and new prior to sale. Apparently many copies were sold with the tissue paper still adhering and this brought forth a disgruntled remark from Frances: "Now *all* the magic book collectors want it with tissue guards!"

Mere readers didn't care whether the tissue was attached or not and, of course, the binder's intention was to have it removed before selling. Frances, too, didn't care—until she began receiving complaints from collectors who were receiving books without them. I remember heading home hoping that the tissue on my copy was still intact. I had become a magic book collector.

What really brought me into the ranks as a collector was following Jay's suggestion (printed on the back cover of the book) to write Gus Rapp to ask for his autograph. This I did, and on the next page is a reduced reproduction of Rapp's letter in reply.

Milwaukee - Wis Jan - 5 - 60

Dear Mr Meyer

Below is the auto. Please excuse delay. Too many holiday activities

Best Wishes

Augustus Rapp

Augustus Rapp.

It was also Jay Marshall who sometime later advised me to keep up my interest in collecting magic books. He said, neither with glee nor with anticipation but as a simple statement of fact, that the collections of older magic enthusiasts would eventually become available to younger collectors like me. What he failed to say, and probably never considered, was that many of these collections would go to him.

One of the finest was that of Arthur H. "Andy" Anderson, who lived on the south side of Chicago. I visited Andy twice and each time considered it a perilous journey getting there. I was still in high school and living in northwest Indiana, and was not familiar with or confident about riding the rapid transit system in the big city. Although I managed to get off at the right station, I remember peering out the window of the train as it swept through hostile-looking neighborhoods and wondering why I hadn't stayed safely at home.

Andy had long been retired when I met him. He was worn and bent and looked to be living in near-poverty, but he was still happy with life. He had held various jobs, the first delivering milk using a horse and buggy. That seemed ancient history to me in 1960 and seems more so now.

Andy's collection consisted of magazines and books on tricks and magic history, all in fine condition. Almost everything he owned he had bought new, when he was a young man. Andy had grown old but his books were in the same condition as when he acquired them. He was particularly proud of those he had purchased from the London magic dealer Will Goldston in the 1920s and '30s. Andy had never been to England, but through correspondence he had dealt directly with Goldston himself. He showed me his file of Goldston letters, catalogs and book prospectuses. Every scrap of paper Goldston had sent, except wrapping paper, Andy had saved.

As vividly as I recall the room where we sat talking, with my eyes mesmerized by the spines of his books in the glass-fronted bookcases, I have only two other memories associated with my visits. The first is of another collector from Indiana who came to see Andy while I was there. This man's visit was not much different from a home invasion. After blustering his way in, he wasted no time on being cordial to Andy or me, but went directly to Andy's bookcase, and pulled out one book and then another, each time asking, "You want to sell this? What d'you want for this one?" Andy was not interested in parting with anything. The books were his lifeblood, a connection to his youth and a reason to take pride in what he had collected. But the intruder had no interest in simply appreciating what Andy had. He soon left, empty-handed and deservedly frustrated.

My other memory has an element of magic to it, but nothing to do with books. Andy had a granddaughter—and grand she was in my view. She was helping Andy's wife in the kitchen the second time I visited. They were sewing or assembling tricks for Ireland Magic Company. Barely into her teens, bright-eyed, blond and decidedly pretty, Andy's granddaughter had her eyes on me as well.

We all had lunch together in their kitchen. I sat across from the sudden girl of my dreams. While Andy talked about magic and magicians, I thought about other things as the girl smiled and flirted. Always slow in my perceptions concerning women, I now wonder—forty years later—if Andy's wife hadn't invited their granddaughter specifically to meet me.

I never saw any of them again, but had a romance bloomed, Andy's pristine magic collection might not have gone to Jay Marshall.

BOOKS
AND
COLLECTORS

Regretting and Getting

EVEN IN THE FIELD of book collecting one manages to collect a few regrets along the way. Most of these are associated with books wanted but missed: the volume lost to another collector because he beat you out on eBay or to the phone to place his order before you received the catalog. Or even more painful, he was the fellow in the shop paying for the book you wanted as you strolled in to look for a copy. There is always the possibility that he will die in your lifetime and his widow will plead with you to haul his stuff away, but that is an unhealthy hope at best. It is more likely another copy will come your way, and this time you will be ahead of someone who had wanted it also. In that case, your regret becomes someone else's.

One of my regrets concerned a copy of *The Fashionable Science of Parlour Magic.* This slim pamphlet was issued by John Henry Anderson (1814–1874), who was born in the north of Scotland and called himself "The Great Wizard of the North," a title which served him well during his many years as a traveling magician—that is, until his appearances in the southern states of America at the outbreak of the Civil War. According to Raymond Toole Stott's *A Bibliography of English Conjuring 1581–1876* (Derby, England, 1976), copies of Anderson's pamphlet, which he sold during his performances, were often printed in the town in which he was appearing. "It is difficult to credit that this work can have run into 250 editions," Toole Stott noted, "but there *is* a 250th edition and it has been specially printed, i.e. not made up of the sheets of previous editions with a new title page." These days it is a scarce and valuable booklet coveted by collectors. The copy I missed was offered in the catalog of an Irish book dealer from whom I had been buying books for years. I frequently wrote notes to him when paying invoices, reminding him to advise me whenever a magic book might come his way. But I had never heard from him in this regard.

When his catalog appeared listing the Anderson book, I was furious—and also eager to reach him by phone. His wife answered, checked the listing and told me the book had been sold. Poor unsuspecting lady! I unleashed my anguish and disappointment over her husband's treatment of a long-time customer. She could only apologize. I harrumphed and hung up.

This incident became a twice-felt regret when I received a letter from the bookseller explaining that the

Anderson had been listed in his last *two* catalogs, both of which he had sent to me. Somehow I had missed its first listing. The second had caught the attention of several others besides me.

To have missed the book by a careless perusal of a catalog was bad enough, but I had the further humbling experience of seeing the book surface in another dealer's catalog only a few months later—at nearly three times the previous price. I relearned a lesson I should never have forgotten: read a book catalog carefully the first time and maybe even twice.

Then there are the regrets one justly deserves for having passed up books which could, at the time, have been easily purchased. What collector hasn't been overtaken by caution with a book in hand, either fairly priced, underpriced or overpriced? All of these scenarios can cause one to instinctively set aside a near-purchase, to wait for another time. This happened to me one year when I flew to Cleveland to attend an antiquarian book show. Someone, and I never found out who, seemed to be ahead of me at every booth where I inquired about magic books.

"I had one," was the reply I kept getting, "but I just sold it."

If a dealer still had a book or two, they were common reprints. At one dealer's booth, however, I came across an intriguing 19th-century English chapbook which lay among pamphlets and ephemera scattered across the table. Titled *Rhyming Dick and the Strolling Player: Being a True Account of the Life and Death of Richard Nancollas,* it was published in Nottingham in the early 1800s, and priced at twenty dollars. Nothing in the text or title indicated any magic interest. What caught my eye was a single woodcut illustration which depicted a man holding a goblet and pointing to it with a wand. Next to him were three more upturned goblets—surely meant for the classic Cups and Balls trick. Or were they?

The illustration seemed to be familiar, yet I was sure I had never actually examined the chapbook before. Twenty dollars was not a steep price for an early imprint, but I said to myself, "I'm thinking this is magic because I've come all the way to Cleveland to buy magic books and there aren't any." If I spent twenty dollars and carried the book home, only to find that I was mistaken, it would merely remind me of a wasted trip to Cleveland and my one foolish purchase. I would want it out of my house in an instant. Why bother if I wasn't sure?

What I needed with me at that moment was Toole Stott's bibliography to confirm my suspicion either way, especially considering that my suspicion kept

RHYMING DICK

AND THE

Strolling Player:

Being a true Account of the Life and Death of

RICHARD NANCOLLAS,

THE ALEHOUSE POET;

AND OF A PORTUGUESE PLAYER,

WHO DIED IN LONDON

With another Narrative, shewing the Advantages of

Societies for visiting the Sick.

NOTTINGHAM:

Printed by C. Sutton, for the Flying Stationers.

The slightly fire-singed front cover of *Rhyming Dick* (c. 1800).

fluctuating. It *was* a magic book. It was *not* a magic book. But I was empty-handed, without the tools of my trade. I looked it over a last time, laid it down, and a few hours later returned home, with no purchases worth remembering.

Several days passed before I thought about the book again and decided to look in Toole Stott's bibliography. There it was, entry 599, which located a copy in London University's Harry Price Library and another in the library of the private English club The Magic Circle. As if that weren't enough evidence, I checked through catalogs of various auction sales of magic collections. A sale conducted by Swann Galleries in New York on June 5, 1986, not only offered a copy but included the cover illustration which I had puzzled over in Cleveland. The Swann copy, described as having the "top 2 inches of inner margin slightly affected by fire," had sold for six hundred and five dollars, including the auctioneer's premium.

The copy I had seen in Ohio had even less of a carbon tinge than the Swann copy. This distinguishing feature suggested that a stack of these books (no doubt a *small* stack, but a stack nevertheless) had been found in some Englishman's attic or bookseller's basement. Perhaps someone had dropped a burning match and this, so to speak, had brought the pile of pamphlets to light. This had certainly occurred with an accumulation of 19th-century broadsides headed "Splendid Amusement! Startling Feats of Legerdemain! Magic! Nose Penetration! Admittance 15 cents" for a magician named "Mr A. Walker" which turned up in New England in the 1980s. The first copy of the broadside which I acquired had a large cigarette burn through it, but its price, around twenty-five dollars, was reasonable considering the defect. A few years later another copy came my way with a smaller burn hole and a larger price. I bought it and gave my first copy to a friend. Finally, I acquired one with no sign of that telltale burn, indicating that it had been near the bottom of the pile. These broadsides continue to be offered now and again, some with holes, others without, but the price has always been more than for the previous one offered.

So *Rhyming Dick* was likely to have come into the market in relatively recent times, although over 175 years after publication. This convinced me—a week too late and 500 miles from where I had spotted it—that I wanted, finally, to acquire it.

I had kept the list of Ohio dealers who had exhibited at the Cleveland book show and sent a letter to those whose specialties were likely to include the chapbook. I enclosed a self-addressed prepaid postcard, asking them to reply, just to confirm that they had never had it—or even that they had had it and sold it. I wrote at least fifteen dealers but only one bothered to reply, wishing me luck at ever finding the book again. That was the end of the story, and another regret added to my collection—or so I thought.

A month later I attended a book show in Chicago and there on a dealer's table, lying like a discarded napkin, was *Rhyming Dick.* It was the same copy I had seen in Ohio. I bought it, of course, with exuberance and without hesitation. The dealer was not one of those whom I had written because he wasn't from Ohio. He came from Michigan and was only an hour-and-a-half drive from where I live. I had visited his shop many times and often since, looking for another rarity at a modest price. You never know what might turn up in Michigan.

STREAKS OF LUCK come in every field of endeavor and often in collecting—although not often enough. My best example followed the sale of the famed Roland Winder collection of conjuring books which took place at Sotheby & Company's auction rooms in London on March 18, 1974. Since that time successive auctions of magic books have eclipsed both the notoriety and the prices attained at the Winder sale, but this auction established a worldwide recognition of magic books which had never previously existed. Two bidders especially, one a general antiquarian book dealer and the other an individual not previously known as a buyer of magic books, helped drive up the prices of the Winder collection. Between them, they acquired 84 of the 230 lots offered.

Roland Winder was a successful English industrialist who had been an amateur magician since his boyhood. He began collecting magic books late in life; but with the advice of the premier collectors of his day—Trevor Hall in England and Milbourne Christopher in the States, to name but two—he acquired a collection which included many rarities. In his *Check List of the Older Books on Conjuring in the Library of Roland Winder as at December, 1966,* given as a Christmas gift to fellow collectors, one finds listed a second edition of *Hocus Pocus Junior* (published in 1635, the first illustrated magic book and one of the rarest), Dean's *The Whole Art of Legerdemain* (which, despite its many editions published in the 18th and 19th centuries and the fact that Winder owned thirteen from the period between 1727 and 1860, is a highly prized and difficult book to acquire), and numerous others that can be best described as "rare." His *Check List* itself, which his friend Hall characteristically described as being issued "in irritating obscurity," has become a much-sought-after, seldom-found title.

My own fascination with Winder's collection began in Jay and Frances Marshall's kitchen in Chicago in April 1974. Jay had recently returned from a trip to England, wisely timed to coincide with the Winder sale at Sotheby's. He had not only been in the auction room, he had opened the bidding on several lots and had tape-recorded portions of the proceedings to prove it. I still recall hearing the voice of the auctioneer on the tape saying, "We begin the bidding at . . . Mr. Marshall bids. . . ." Of the two hundred and thirty lots offered, Jay was chagrined at having successfully purchased only four. As I listened, with excitement and envy, I felt Jay to be fortunate indeed, for I had never even had a chance to bid. I had missed one of the great sales of conjuring literature of the 20th century.

In the spring of 1976, however, two years to the very month after the auction, some incredible luck began coming my way—initially in the form of a crudely typed, mimeographed catalog from a New England book dealer. His catalog listed a hodgepodge of material, from 17th-century books in bad condition to modern works at cheap prices, with an occasional engraving, handwritten farmer's journal or some other odd item thrown in. The gem (at least to me) in the

March 1976 catalog was a copy of Badcock's *Domestic Amusements, or Philosophical Recreations,* printed in London about 1825 and handsomely rebound in modern half morocco. Its only illustration is a fold-out colored plate titled "Aquatic Tripod" showing a gentleman in high hat and leggings shooting at wildfowl while paddling through a pond on a contraption sure to scatter birds half a mile ahead and likely to cause a groin injury on either the mount or dismount. The magic section is devoted to "amusing and ingenious tricks and contrivances." No mention was made of this charmer having come from the Roland Winder collection; I learned that when the book arrived by mail. It had been Lot 18.

The following month's catalog from the same dealer offered another copy of *Domestic Amusements,* bound in three-quarter morocco with raised bands on the spine and top edge gilt. It was a presentation copy from Trevor Hall to Roland Winder and had been Lot 17 in the sale.

Over the next several months, from different dealers in the States and England, I acquired two copies of another Badcock book—*Philosophical Recreations, or Winter Amusements* (London, c. 1802), one in original boards and the other rebound in half morocco—which had appeared in Winder's Lots 15 and 16.

These books, attractive as they are with their fold-out, hand-colored frontispieces, are not particularly rare. Yet what seems remarkable to me even now is that on checking the Winder auction catalog, I found that I owned every Badcock volume which had been auctioned from Winder's collection, and they had come from different sources.

If only my luck could continue! I began to think it might. Several months followed without acquiring a single Winder title. Then a copy of the first edition of *Endless Amusement* turned up in an English dealer's catalog. Published in London about 1815 and subtitled *A collection of upwards of 400 entertaining and astonishing experiments,* this copy was finely rebound in modern half morocco. I knew immediately by the description of the binding that I was again on the Winder trail. Difficult as it is to believe in these days of instant e-mail, I wrote a letter (instead of calling overseas) to order the book and still managed to obtain it.

Perhaps in the overconfidence that precedes a fall, I remember checking the Winder auction catalog to see what other copies of *Endless Amusement* might turn up. Lots 68 and 69 had offered single copies of early editions of the book and Lot 70 had been composed of various imperfect editions and sequels—nine copies in that lot alone!

But my luck ran out after I acquired Lot 68, a very good copy of the second edition in its original boards. Attached to the inside front cover are the bookplates of Roland Winder and the English collector Graham Adams, who apparently bought it from the London book dealer who acquired it at Sotheby's.

I purchased the book neither from an English nor a New England bookseller, but much closer to home: in the antiquarian book department of Marshall Field's department store in Chicago.

I haven't acquired a book from the Winder collection since. But for someone who never placed a bid at the auction, I could say I did quite well.

Houdini—Lost and Found

THE LITERATURE on the life and career of Harry Houdini seems boundless. Since his death in 1926 enough biographies of the escape artist and magician have appeared to fill several bookshelves. These include a handful of serious studies and a multitude of sketchy and mostly pictorial books which recount his famous feats. (One of these is actually a cartoon depiction of his life. Is there a greater level of fame in popular culture than to become a cartoon?) A growing number of fictional works also include Houdini and Houdini-like characters. Houdini himself, long gone, seems destined to have his life repeated over and over again as new books about him continue to appear.

This brings to mind all the *un*finished Houdini projects which must have been undertaken in the decades since his death. They, too, might be characterized as boundless, in more ways than one. I refer to such projects for a soon-to-be-obvious reason. I am thinking of thirty years ago—or about a shelf and a half fewer Houdini books than exist today.

Several years after the publication of Milbourne

Christopher's 1969 biography, *Houdini: The Untold Story*, my friend Jay Marshall had the idea of compiling a day-to-day chronology of Houdini's life. It was an interesting project as it seemed possible to track Houdini's career by the mass of information which had been printed about him. His escapes, publicity stunts, performances and tangles with spiritualists were often described in detail in newspaper stories, magazine features and promotional materials. Much of what might seem to have been lost through the ravages of time was still in existence and accessible.

Jay had friends who owned scrapbooks which Houdini had compiled during his lifetime. They cover the important early periods of Houdini's career: the first years of struggle in dime museums through the record-breaking years of success in England and Germany. Assembled with the industry and enthusiasm of a young performer determined to build on his every success, these scrapbooks carry almost daily accounts of where Houdini was and what he was up to.

Jay also had the perfect person to undertake his project, a fellow interested in Houdini's career, who was out of work and needed some focus in his life, and who happened to own Houdini's scrapbook covering the period 1900 to 1905. This fellow was me.

Jay had begun the project by jotting down dates on

scraps of white fiberboard. After moving into a second-floor back bedroom of Magic, Inc., the home and business of Jay and Frances Marshall, and finding a place to work within the shadow of many bookshelves, I took up the challenge with pencil and note cards.

Our project progressed for several months, albeit with frequent interruptions as I joined Jay in attending a book sale or visiting an old book shop or lunching with an out-of-town magician. In between jaunts I managed to fill a long tray with cards detailing dates, places, performances, occurrences and names. In addition to the scrapbooks which we had photocopied, Jay piled on brochures, articles, letters and other ephemera pertaining to Houdini's life. My task was simple enough: put it in order, write it down, file it.

I had begun working in the late fall of 1973. The following spring Jay flew to England to perform in several shows (and attend book sales, visit book shops and be a visiting magician himself). When he returned a month later he had another Houdini project in mind. Actually, this second project had been brewing while I had been working on the first. The widow of John Mulholland, the longtime editor of the magic magazine *The Sphinx,* owned a recording of Houdini speaking—the only copy of the one instance when Houdini's voice had been captured on an Edison cylinder. Jay purchased this treasure and asked me to write a script to go with it. We were going to become record producers. Thus the day-to-day chronology of Houdini's career came to an end, long before its completion. The script for a record never really began. I just didn't have the talent for it.

All of this is but a prelude to what I am about to relate. In the spring of 1990 the Neil See Collection, a large assemblage of magic books, was auctioned in New York City. The sale offered a few rarities and many standard magic books and periodicals in English and foreign languages. The most remarkable thing about the sale was the interest it generated. The run-up in prices of magic books and memorabilia had been steadily increasing over the years and this phenomenon had brought more and more people into the field who could be best described as investors rather than collectors. Many of these people bid at the sale.

When the list of prices paid was issued several weeks after the auction, it became obvious that although a few items sold at their everyday values, the majority of successful bidders had to pay premium prices.

Seventeen lots contained books written by or about Harry Houdini. The most common item in this group was the forty-page booklet titled *Houdini Exposes the tricks used by the Boston Medium "Margery,"* printed in New York in 1924. For decades original copies of this booklet were to be found by the dozen, gathering dust in magic shops across the country. They started disappearing in the 1960s. From the usual dollar-a-copy, the price soared to ten dollars, later to twenty or more.

Two lots in the auction offered copies of this booklet. (I wondered at the time: What happened to the other ten copies in the pile? And why weren't these two described as "dusty"?) The auction catalog's suggested amount for successfully bidding on *each* of these copies was—*not* $10—*not* $20—but $100 to $150! Who would have guessed that the fires of auction fever would set these two ablaze? The first copy sold for $523 and the second for $660!

Another notable and, in this instance, scarce Houdini item in the auction was *Yar, The Primeval Man.* Printed in 1921, the twelve-page pamphlet contains a story idea for a film which Houdini evidently hoped to star in. (This was yet another Houdini project which was never completed.) Houdini protected his creative property by publishing and copyrighting his story. If there were any dusty stacks of *this* pamphlet lying around, they hadn't been found, at least not recently. The damp-stained copy offered in the Neil See auction sold for $935.

Printed with pink covers and selling for a dollar in 1924, "*Margery*" remained unchanged in price (and most of the copies unsold) for the next fifty years. Once an auctioneer boosted the price by six hundred percent, the booklet became a luxury item.

Jay phoned me soon after receiving the list of prices realized at the auction.

"You know I own a copy of *Yar,*" he said. "But I can't find it."

Considering that Jay's collection—a *university* of specialized collections is a more proper description—encompassed numerous rooms in Magic, Inc., and most of two adjoining buildings, I was surprised that he could even remember owning the booklet. I recalled having seen it once, and it had been in fine condition—not a mere damp-stained nine-hundred-dollar copy.

"I haven't seen it for a couple years," Jay said.

As we talked my memory slipped back to that niche in the book-filled room above his magic shop. *Yar* had been among the booklets which Jay had brought me while I was working on the Houdini chronology. It had lain for months among the other materials which littered my desk. When I left Magic, Inc., in the mid-70s, I had taken along the tray of file cards and the folders of photocopies from the Houdini project. These I had stored in the bottom drawer of a wooden filing cabinet in my basement and never really looked at since.

"I think I know where your copy of *Yar* might be," I said. "Let me look and I'll call you later."

I went downstairs to the old cabinet and there, among other pamphlets I had consulted, safely tucked away in a browned folder, was Jay's pristine copy of *Yar, The Primeval Man.* I hesitated before calling him. Surely he would be elated to hear that it was found again. He would have to be amused to learn that instead of having lost track of the book for "a couple years," in fact he had not seen his *Yar* in fifteen years.

But although he might never say so, I was sure it would cross his mind that maybe—just maybe—I had known *Yar* was there all that time.

Who wouldn't wonder that?

Dealing with Dr. Hall

THE CLOSEST I ever came to owning a world-class collection of conjuring books began with my correspondence with Dr. Trevor H. Hall of England, a noted writer, historian and lecturer in several fields. Hall's many accomplishments are best summed up in an obituary which appeared in the London *Times* following his death at the age of eighty in 1991.

"Because of his wide variety of interests," the obituary began, "Dr. Hall will be remembered by many people for different reasons. As a writer on Sherlock Holmes, Trevor Hall was regarded by some quarters as the most elegant exponent of the higher criticism of the literature of Baker Street. . . . But perhaps his greatest impact was his critical psychical research, particularly that which set out to debunk the myth of Borley Rectory, which had become celebrated in the 1930s as a place of quite remarkable supernatural phenomena. This had come about through a series of experiments conducted by Harry Price, a ghost hunter and investigator of mediums, whose book *The Most Haunted House in England* made Borley a Mecca for seekers after the supernatural. In two books, *The Haunting of Borley Rectory* [co-authored with two others in 1956] and *Search for Harry Price* (1978), Hall effectively demolished any idea that Borley had really been haunted, substituting for the notion a fairly conclusive picture of Price as a hoaxer. There were those who felt the nature of the debunking represented by these two scholarly volumes was perhaps using a sledgehammer to crack a nut. . . ."

Another interest of Dr. Hall's was magic. He had written nearly a dozen books and monographs on the subject, although when I began corresponding with him in 1977, he had essentially put magic behind him. He had been a member of The Magic Circle, the prestigious London association of magicians, for nearly forty years, but would soon resign his membership. Most of his friendships among magicians and magic collectors had already ended. I had been warned by a fellow collector to be cautious in any dealings with him.

In magic Trevor Hall had two reputations: one as a scholar, the other as a scoundrel. I became acquainted with both.

As a scholar he can be credited with having produced the most in-depth and meticulously researched studies of conjuring books that are ever likely to be written. His 1972 treatise, *Old Conjuring Books: A Biblio-*

Frontispiece portrait of Trevor H. Hall, M.A., Ph.D., from his *Old Conjuring Books: A Bibliographical and Historical Study with a Supplementary Check-List* (London and New York, 1976).

graphical and Historical Study, in a limited and signed edition of one thousand copies, was published in London by Duckworth and in New York by St. Martin's Press, both well-known trade publishers. To produce a work which was both scholarly and on the esoteric subject of old magic books and have it issued by two mainstream publishing houses certainly attests to the stature of Trevor Hall as an author and a scholar.

Eight chapters are devoted to describing in detail every major edition of the rarest and most important early books on magic. Rid's *The Art of Jugling* and *Mathematical Recreations* (1633), to name but two of the most important, are scrutinized with a seriousness never given in any previous work. Hall endeavors to reveal their often complicated and confusing origins and to identify and establish long-debated authorships.

The final chapter, "Libraries and Collectors," serves an entirely different purpose, for it is an assemblage of disparaging comments and complaints about several fellow collectors—a few of whom helped Hall form his own collection.

In this chapter he attacks Stanley Collins, described by Hall as "the self-styled possessor of the largest collection of rare conjuring books in Great Britain." Collins, who had earned his living as a private entertainer in the early decades of the 20th century, had been a collector all his life and had known many of the great performers of his time. He often referred to rare books and original manuscripts from his collection in the articles he wrote and the monthly column he contributed to the magic periodical *The Linking Ring*.

But Hall attempted to demolish Collins' reputation as a major collector. What was Collins' crime? In Hall's opinion it was that Collins had engaged in "extensive and secret book dealing." Of course, collectors engage in private dealings, both buying and selling, all the time. But for Collins to sell items from his collection in his lifetime—probably reluctantly because of necessity in his old age—Hall found that reprehensible. Hall also found, as did many other collectors who rushed in to buy books from Collins' widow, that by the time of Collins' death, the size and value of his collection had been greatly depleted. Because of this Hall claimed that Collins never had much in the first place. He was wrong in this regard and he knew it.

Many collectors benefited from Collins' selling. From 1959 through 1963, when I was a teenager, I bought nearly a hundred books from Collins, including a wealth of printed ephemera on Houdini and his rival escape artists, material which I have never seen offered by any dealer or at any auction since. I only wish my knowledge and taste in collecting had been more developed so that I could have obtained the scarcer magic titles which Collins undoubtedly had. One person who did was the late Robert Lund, founder and proprietor of the American Museum of Magic in Marshall, Michigan. Lund told me that many of the rarest and most desirable books in his library had come from Stanley Collins—undoubtedly the same books which Trevor Hall had hoped to acquire.

A great deal of controversy surrounded the 1957 publication of Trevor Hall's *Bibliography of Conjuring Books in English from 1580 to 1850.* This was the basic reference used by collectors for the next two decades. It was an idea promoted by the American collector H. Adrian Smith. Based on the catalog of Smith's own library, the bibliography developed into a collaborative project which tapped the resources of several private collections in England and America. The British collectors Herbert E. Pratt, Chris Charlton and James B. Findlay were among those who worked on the bibliography. All received scant acknowledgment once the project fell into Trevor Hall's hands. The sole holdout among potential contributors was Stanley Collins, an act which damaged his reputation as a collector at the time, and one for which Hall obviously never forgave him.

The publication history of Hall's bibliography is a complicated one and as all of the participants are now dead, the complete story may never be known. However, the matter is discussed in letters of Bert Pratt, one of the contributors who had been brushed aside once the project came to Hall. From the outset the publisher was to be Carl Waring Jones, scion of a wealthy newspaper family in Minneapolis. Jones's hobby was magic and he had already published many well-known magic books, including the classic *Greater Magic.*

Jones was gravely ill by the time the bibliography was completed and ready to be printed. He had originally contracted to publish the book for Smith, then for the group of collectors mentioned above, then for Hall alone. Jones, who did not live to see the book into print, died believing that he was the sole publisher. Yet while Jones was still alive, Hall (who was seeing Jones's edition through the press in England) quietly arranged for his own publication of the bibliography by an English publisher.

The prospectus for Hall's edition, which was virtually identical in content to Jones's (including the paper it was printed on), described the book as being printed on "art paper [and] bound in scarlet boards with strong black buckram spine, titled in gold." (Jones's edition was bound in plain green boards with a cream cloth spine stamped in black.) As an additional inducement to collectors, the English edition was limited to 250 copies, each numbered and signed by Hall. (Jones's edition consisted of 500 copies, neither numbered nor signed.) The "probable publication" date was announced as June 1957. (Jones died in January 1957.) Hall's prospectus also advised that "this strictly limited edition is liable to be heavily over-subscribed," the inference being that buyers should not hesitate to reserve their copies.

Hall effectively killed any chance of Jones's edition selling in England and, with his signed edition of 250 copies, no doubt satisfied the very limited market for the bibliography. Soon after Jones's edition was received from the bindery in England, the heirs of his estate liquidated the entire shipment by selling copies in lots to various magic book dealers in the States. In 1980, twenty years after its publication, I bought the last remaining lot of 100 copies from a dealer in Baltimore.

This is what I knew about Trevor Hall before writing to him: In addition to being a noted collector, scholar and author, he was also a man who apparently walked away from friendships when he had taken what he wanted from them and, if he did not get what he wanted, he was likely to complain in print. He was a formidable character indeed.

One of the more readable titles by Hall is a monograph he wrote in 1975, titled *The Winder Sale of Old Conjuring Books.* It is a thorough and valuable account of the books sold at auction from Roland Winder's famous collection, and the unprecedented prices they realized at Sotheby's auction rooms in London in 1974. Hall correctly infers that the sale ushered in a new awareness of the collectibility and value of old conjuring books.

It was my efforts to obtain copies of this booklet for resale which led me to contact Hall directly in May 1977. I initially purchased five copies and in March 1978 I ordered ten more. Hall responded with this key statement:

"If I was a shrewd person with an eye to the main chance, I suppose that I would hold on to the remaining copies of *The Winder Sale* with the idea that in five years they will have become expensive collectors' items." Although he did sell me these copies and more, I consider Hall's statement a landmark clue to his character.

Regarding these monographs, I won't hesitate to mention a curious oversight of Hall's which he surely would have pounced upon had someone else committed such an error. On the copyright page of *The Winder Sale* is printed this statement: "This is a limited edition of 250 signed and numbered copies. . . ." And following that, in Hall's handwriting, is the designated number of the copy with Hall's signature. However, a printer cannot stop the presses at exactly the number of books called for. The press run usually exceeds the number required to ensure that an order is filled. With an announced limited and numbered edition such as Hall's monograph of 250 copies, the usual practice is to designate extra copies in one of several ways. They can be marked not with a number but with the notation "review copy" and sent out for that purpose. Or they can be noted as "author's copy" or "out of series" and sold as such.

What did Trevor Hall do? He gave the excess copies the same numbers which he had given earlier copies. Thus I purchased two copies of *The Winder Sale* which were numbered "86." If Hall had spotted this telltale detail in anyone else's work, he would have treated it as incriminating evidence of fraud. I've taken a friendlier stance by suggesting that maybe he simply lost count.

In his letter to me of 12 May 1978 he wrote: "I did a deal with [noted New York collector] Morris Young to enable the Library of Congress to possess my duplicate of Neve's book *Hocus Pocus* [published in 1721]. Among the duplicates that I took in the exchange was a fine copy . . . of *Ventriloquism Explained: and Juggler's Tricks or Legerdemain Exposed* [published in] Amherst in 1834. This copy bears my book-plate of thirty years ago, and is available if you wish to make a bid for it."

I bid fifty pounds. Hall accepted my offer. I also bid fifteen pounds for a duplicate copy of Hall's limited, signed edition of his bibliography. "I am not happy . . . with fifteen pounds," he replied. "So let us leave it. I hate bargaining."

In 1969 a monograph had been issued which eventually became a chapter in Hall's *Old Conjuring Books.* Titled *Mathematicall Recreations: An Exercise in Seventeenth Century Bibliography,* this pamphlet was published by The School of English of the University of Leeds. The study dealt with the authorship of a book which was first published in 1633 and which, in its various editions, was attributed to no fewer than three different authors. Hall's monograph was printed in a limited edition of only 200 copies. Having been printed by a university press as a study in textual criticism, few copies found their way into magic collections. Even more uncommon are the four hardcover copies of this work. They came to me in this way: In June 1978 Hall wrote, "I have four unsewn copies . . . , without covers. . . . The idea was to have these cloth or leather bound, out of series and specially numbered, for friends. I never got round to it. Could you use these four unbound copies at say half-price, to have bound up in boards as collectors items?" Yes, I certainly could use them and at ten pounds for the lot, I was glad to get them.

Thus far, all my transactions with Trevor Hall had been easy and pleasant. This was accomplished, in part, by our long-distance rapport based on a mutual interest in his work. He was involved at the time in numerous projects. Several of his earlier books on psychical research were being reprinted. His new book, *Sherlock Holmes and his Creator,* was about to be published and he was already engaged in writing a study of the famous British mystery writer Dorothy L. Sayers. I expressed an interest—a genuine interest, I might add—in all that he was doing, and from my side of the Atlantic I was often able to tell him of the American appearances of his books as they were published. I also sent him reviews and notices whenever I could.

In July 1978 he wrote, "I am much interested in completing my collection of Dorothy L. Sayers detective stories in first editions, either English or American. If you can find any of these I shall be extremely vulnerable to exchanges for a few old conjuring books I have in duplicate, one example being *Holiday Frolics* [which was] illustrated in [the book] *Some Printers and Publishers* [*of Conjuring Books*] by Percy H. Muir and myself."

Locating mystery books was not one of my usual pursuits in the book trade, yet I was eager to undertake the task because of Hall's tempting offer. Although not knowing how easy or difficult Sayers' books were to obtain, I was certainly aware that the reward was worth some effort. *Holiday Frolics,* published in London in 1830, was a slight book in itself, but it was also rare and, with its double hand-colored frontispiece, rather lovely. Its title reads in part *Holiday Frolics or Endless Amusement for the Christmas Fireside. Containing, the most astonishing feats of legerdemain, and astounding conjurings; Entertaining experiments in various branches of science; Tricks with Cards & Dice. Art of making fireworks,* [etc.].

When Raymond Toole Stott was preparing his 1976 *Bibliography of English Conjuring,* he was able to locate only three copies of *Holiday Frolics*—one in The Library of Congress, the second in the Magic Circle Library and the third in the collection of H. Adrian Smith. No other major collector of magic books apparently owned a copy at that time. Trevor Hall owned *two* copies and he was offering one to me.

I immediately placed ads in the trade journal *Antiquarian Bookman* seeking Sayers first editions. I also wrote letters to dealers who specialized in buying and selling mystery books. Then I sat back to await the results—and to think about that copy of *Holiday Frolics* which would soon be sitting on my bookshelf. But in late September, after failing to receive a single response to any of my ads or a reply from the nearly twenty dealers who might have Sayers titles, I wrote Hall: "I am finding that these items are very difficult to come by. . . . I will keep advertising and inquiring, of course—and hoping you will, in any event, hold on to *Holiday Frolics* so that I will somehow manage to acquire it for my collection."

"Rest assured," he replied, "that *Holiday Frolics* will remain on *my* shelf until something comes up, as it assuredly must sometime."

In December I wrote: "The Dorothy L. Sayers books continue to be a total mystery. I make inquiries, I advertise, and I still have come up with nothing you seek. I have never found an author's work to be so elusive!"

But while I, the book dealer, was coming up empty-handed, Trevor Hall the book collector was not. In mid-January 1979 he advised me that an English bookseller had just sent him a first American edition of

Sayers' *The Documents in the Case,* for the moderate sum of seven pounds. "I now have both the English and American firsts of this quite rare book," Hall wrote, "which will certainly go up in value when my [new book on Dorothy L.] Sayers [is] published."

While I was complaining, Hall was rejoicing!

Finally, in February, I had some success.

"So it looks as if you have located two first [American editions] for me," he wrote, "at a total of thirty-two dollars and fifty cents or about sixteen pounds in English money, which seems very fair to me."

Six months had passed and I was not much closer to my prize. I tried another tack.

"I wonder if I might not come closer to effecting a trade for your duplicate copy of *Holiday Frolics,*" I wrote, "by offering my services for obtaining other books for you as well."

As examples I suggested recent books and a bibliography on Sayers which I secretly hoped he did not have but needed for the writing of his own book. He quickly replied that there were no current books in America which he wanted. And if that weren't enough of a setback, a dealer who had offered me a Sayers first edition which Hall wanted returned my check. As if on the same wavelength as Hall, he decided that the Sayers book would soon increase in value and he didn't want to part with it after all! So, after nine months of diligent searching, I had come up with only one book—worth twelve pounds fifty pence in credit—toward Hall's *Holiday Frolics.*

By April 1979 I had again made some progress and could send him a second book for a total of twenty-five pounds in my favor. By then I realized that while Hall and I were putting values on the books I was sending him, Hall had not suggested the value in trade for which he was willing to turn over his book to me.

"You ask me for my view of a fair price for *Holiday Frolics,*" he wrote. "The copy ear-marked for you is in excellent condition. The Winder sale, although now five years out of date, is the only guide we have to price. If you glance at my little book on the sale and what I paid for this type of rare item you will agree that *Holiday Frolics* must be worth sixty pounds or one hundred twenty dollars."

Ah, those hypnotic words of Hall's—"You will agree!" He was to use that phrase in his letters to me many times.

"On questions of money," he wrote in July 1979, "the British pound is on the move, but as we are on a friendly basis I suggest that we agree on two dollars to the pound whatever variations take place."

I was also on the move and by late August had turned up three more first editions which Hall had been seeking for his collection. The prices I had paid for these books brought my total credit with Hall to sixty-four pounds—four pounds *over* the value he had placed on *Holiday Frolics.* I wrote Hall a long letter describing the books I had for him and advised him that these books would consummate our trade.

Hall's previous letter to me had been written on July 5th, the day of the first sale of the famous J. B. Findlay collection of magic books, posters and catalogs at Sotheby's. As with the Winder sale, it turned out to be a fateful day for the pocketbooks of all magic collectors.

Hall had told me that he had a "rolling bid" for four rare books from the Findlay collection and—as he phrased it—"I am bound to pick up something." But in his next letter he wrote, "Even with a rolling bid totalling four hundred pounds I failed to get anything—the four items I wanted all being early nineteenth century booklets. It was on the basis of the Winder prices that I put *Holiday Frolics* at sixty pounds, but"—and here's that dreaded phrase once again—"you will be the first to agree that with the new evidence now available, [*Holiday Frolics*] must be worth at least three times that figure."

Three times sixty pounds! Suddenly my paltry credit wasn't going to get the prize.

Scarce and rare conjuring books are selling for thousands of dollars these days. A few hundred dollars seems insignificant in comparison. But in 1979 nearly two hundred English pounds and twice that in dollars were record prices for such books. In those days, too, I had more youth than money—a situation which has since reversed.

Because it was obvious to Hall that the five Sayers books I had sent him did not add up to the increased value of *Holiday Frolics,* he suggested I simply send him a bill for the books. Or, if I did agree with him that the Findlay sale had rendered the Winder prices obsolete—and who could disagree with the facts?—*and* I cared to suggest a new price for *Holiday Frolics,* he would give it his consideration. He promised to keep in mind our valued friendship and all the efforts I had taken to find Sayers books for him.

By then I had acquired five more Sayers first editions which he had been seeking. I described them carefully to Hall in my letter of August 29th. Previously I had offered him books at the prices I had paid for them. This time I did *not* put prices on the books. I must have finally started thinking in a Trevor Hall–like manner.

My letter crossed in the mails with his letter of September 1st, in which he stated, "I am of the firm belief that if Findlay had possessed a copy of *Holiday Frolics* it would have brought at least two hundred pounds. . . ." He went on to say that he did not expect me to offer as much as he thought the book was now worth, but some "modestly increased offer" would act as a token that the Findlay sale had come as a surprise to both of us.

The price, in his mind, obviously kept rising. As it rose, so rose my anger and so fell my faith in ever acquiring *Holiday Frolics* from Trevor Hall.

Another segment of the Findlay collection was coming up for sale within a few weeks and I knew that it would only further convince him to keep raising the price. So I did not answer his two letters of September and I did not expect to correspond with him again.

On December 5th he wrote, "I have heard nothing from you for a period of over three months. . . . I cannot think that you can have taken offence at what I said about *Holiday Frolics* in my letter of September. I believe that my suggestion that you might wish to make a modestly increased offer for *Holiday Frolics* . . . was entirely fair. Nothing was further from my mind than that you should pay two hundred pounds or anything like it."

Why did Hall back down on his previously "firm belief" that I *should* pay a Findlay price for *Holiday Frolics?*

The answer came in the postscript to this letter. "Looking back on your letter of August 29th," he added, "I think that if you had offered to obtain for me the five unpriced [Sayers books] mentioned, I would have agreed and sent you *Holiday Frolics* by air. You would have gained heavily, but the principle would have been accepted that the Findlay sale must be looked at, however slightly."

I had acquired a measure of disgust for this drawn-out affair and Hall's changes of mind, but I wrote politely, "I must admit that I was a bit disconcerted by your revised estimate on the *Holiday Frolics* after believing we had struck a firm bargain on its value for purposes of trading. This is not to say that I do not appreciate your position in the matter. . . ."

I then explained why he should appreciate *my* position. I had offered him the Sayers books at the same prices I had paid for them—wholesale prices, not retail prices, not auction room prices. I had also not added in my costs for advertising, my efforts spent in contacting book dealers and my costs in sending him the books. I finally told him that if he would airmail me his copy of *Holiday Frolics,* I would send him the five

Frontispiece (hand-colored) from *Holiday Frolics* (London, 1830).

first editions. He mailed the book to me on January 10, 1980.

What happened next can only be termed a collector's chance of a lifetime—though to this very day I doubt I ever really had such a chance. One might call this a postscript to the *Holiday Frolics* affair and aptly title it "Hall's Revenge."

In the same letter in which he acknowledged sending me *Holiday Frolics* he wrote, "I have been wondering seriously about selling my collection of conjuring books. I have written all I intend to write on the subject. In my seventieth year I have to think seriously about the possibility of leaving my wife with a complicated asset over which she might be cheated through her entire lack of knowledge of the subject. My collection fills only two book shelves, since so many of the rare items in the first half of the nineteenth century are small and thin, and I think it fair to say that starting from the first edition of Scot [*Discoverie of Witchcraft,* published in 1584] in vellum, it contains nearly every rarity of note through to 1850. Indeed, when I started the collection the rough guide was to be that every item would be one that would cause a visiting collector to cross himself reverently when it was placed in his hands!"

The Findlay sale had brought forth previously unbelievable prices for old magic books, even books in bad condition. Hall obviously saw this as his "main chance" to dispose of his library at the best price possible—and he acted swiftly.

"In a couple of days," he wrote in his next letter to

me, a book dealer friend was coming "to discuss the possible sale of my collection intact to an American university." This letter was dated March 6th. Two days later he followed with another reporting that his dealer friend had a client who was willing to buy his collection at any price the dealer recommended up to a certain amount.

"To help me decide," he wrote, "will you say (a) whether you would be interested and (b) whether we are likely to agree on a price."

Question A was easy enough to answer: I was certainly interested. But after all the wrangling over *Holiday Frolics,* the answer to Question B was anyone's guess.

I asked him to send me a list of his books and soon received a thirteen-page manuscript describing in detail 150 of the choicest and rarest conjuring books one is ever likely to see in several lifetimes, including:

Eight different editions of *Breslaw's Last Legacy; or, The Magical Companion: Containing all that is Curious, Pleasing, Entertaining, and Comical; Selected from the most celebrated Masters of Deception,* [etc.], published in London between 1784 and 1800. This book and the one following fall into a class of "popular street literature"—books which were, in the words of a knowledgeable bibliographer, literally "thumbed out of existence."

Fifteen different editions of one of the most prized books in magic, Henry Dean's *Whole Art of Legerdemain or Hocus Pocus in Perfection,* from the second edition of 1727 to the 1886 Glasgow edition, plus another ten books of the 17th and 18th centuries which employed variations on this title.

A fine copy of the extremely rare *Hocus Pocus Junior,* one of only two known copies in private hands. This is the book which, sixty years before, a prominent dealer called "the hope and the despair of the seeker after rare magic books." Hall also owned five other early books with "Hocus Pocus" in their titles.

Three different editions of Thomas Hill's 18th-century rarity, *Legerdemain or Natural and Artificial Conclusions.*

Also four editions of John White's *A Rich Cabinet,* a fascinating compendium of secrets and recipes, including magic tricks, which were printed in London in 1658, 1684 and 1710.

One of the four existing copies of Sidney W. Clarke's monumental history *The Annals of Conjuring,* which were specially printed and bound by the publisher George Johnson. Hall owned Johnson's personal copy.

These are all rare books in the truest sense of the word, and 103 others on Hall's list, at the very least, fall into the category of scarce and desirable. All were described as in fine condition.

I spent several frantic days devising ways to justify offering seventy thousand dollars for Hall's library, although I wasn't at all certain that this would be the final figure. A bookseller friend agreed to participate in the financing, which meant that some of the best books would have to be sold to recoup his investment. I tried to keep in mind that whatever books I could finally keep for myself would be better than not having any at all.

In retrospect, I now believe Hall never seriously considered selling the collection to me. I was, more or less, a sounding board—someone to write to as he thrashed out his ideas on how to best dispose of his collection. In a series of letters that followed one upon another he told me that his dealer friend had had lunch with the directors of Sotheby's in London and they wanted to auction his books if he provided a preface for the sale catalog. Soon after he advised that a client had offered him a figure far greater than my estimate—"but," he wrote, "I think this may be increased."

He had received my telegram attempting to set a date to come to England to make an offer, but that possibility ended with a quick reply that the library had been sold. He described the transaction in this way: "I appreciate your interest, but you will understand the attraction of my dealing with a local man who will simply put the books in his enormous Mercedes Benz and take them off to the castle he owns fifty miles from here."

It was true that the buyer lived in a castle. But this wonderful collection of books did not stay there for long. Several years later I learned that they had been sent to a London book dealer. By the time I contacted this firm the collection had been sold again. Someone later hinted to me that the collection had gone to California.

Then one day Jay Marshall phoned me from a place he was visiting in Kansas and began describing 18th-century conjuring books which he was looking at as he spoke—and which he thought would make me squirm. The book titles and their descriptions sounded suspiciously familiar. He said the books had come from California, were in the hands of a dealer and on their way to a wealthy collector in France. Were they Trevor Hall's books? I couldn't say for sure, although each time I recall the telephone conversation, I experience a sense of loss and frustration.

Wherever Trevor Hall's collection may be now, how it got there is someone else's story.

Postscript to the Hall Affair

IN 1986 I COMPOSED and published a slim monograph with the long-winded title *LEGERDEMAIN, Or SLEIGHT of HAND: A facsimile reproduction with plates from the third edition (1797) of the ENCYCLOPAEDIA BRITANNICA with an essay on its origins and a guide to its appearances in all editions.*

For years I'd had on my library shelves the twenty-page treatise "Legerdemain, or Sleight of Hand," extracted from the third edition of the *Encyclopaedia Britannica* (1788–1797). It is a thorough and intriguing article offering detailed explanations of the various classic effects in magic: the Cups and Balls, performances with cards, and miscellaneous tricks using apparatus, optical effects and sympathetic inks. It is, in the words of magic scholar Edgar Heyl, "a representative picture of what constituted conjuring in the latter part of the 18th century."

Many collectors with whom I had discussed this treatise had said to me, "Oh, I have that!"—when, in fact, many of them did not have the one identical to mine. As I was to learn, several versions of the treatise had been published over a period of fifty-five years in five different editions of the *Encyclopaedia.*

I thought the treatise was important and interesting enough to merit a facsimile reprinting. I thought, too, that a listing of all its appearances in the *Encyclopaedia* would be enlightening, especially for those who thought they owned the one and only version. This would be a good project for a professional bibliographer; a man who also had some stature in the field of magic history would undoubtedly add to the appeal of the book.

I wrote to Dr. Trevor Hall, asking if he would be interested in writing an introduction to my work. For a certain sum in pounds sterling, he agreed. Unfortunately, he either misunderstood my requirements or simply wasn't up to the task. He wrote not about the treatise but about himself and his experiences in preparing his own books, which he considered to be the hallmark for all works on the subject. As the essay consisted mainly of passages extracted from his previously published books, I could not use it. This was doubly unfortunate considering the amount of money I had paid him in advance.

The next fellow for the job came more reluctantly but much cheaper . . . I did not consider myself qualified, much less adept at bibliographical research, but I decided that if I made careful notes and checked everything twice, how could I fail? Having the world headquarters of Encyclopaedia Britannica, Inc. in Chicago, only an hour's drive from my office, was also in my favor. However, the company's reference library, used only by their staff, was not open to the public. Fortunately, the day I phoned the librarian to ask the favor of checking their collection of every edition of the *Encyclopaedia* from the first to the current edition, she was in a good mood and said, "Okay." I may have foolishly indicated that I would need only an hour or two, but I stayed the entire day. Then I asked to come back. Perhaps I should have told the librarian how much more material I found than I had expected, for one source inevitably gave hint of another source in another edition. As it turned out, my search led all the way from a wordy 18th-century patter for the Cups and Balls, to John Nevil Maskelyne, of London's Egyptian Hall theatre fame, telling why he and the French magicians Robert-Houdin and Buatier De Kolta were the only true originators in magic in the 19th century, to Houdini declaring that his success in escapes was based in part on his being bowlegged, to magician John Mulholland covering magic's entire history in a short, precise and scholarly essay. There was much magic to be found in the pages of the *EB*.

Again and again, after each visit, I found myself asking the librarian if I could come back one more time; and, less and less friendly each time, she continued to say, "Okay." The last time I asked—luckily over the telephone—she finally had had enough of me. She reminded me of my first request for a few hours' visit and how it had stretched into days. She said she had watched me "skulking around the stacks." She didn't know exactly what I was up to but she made a wild guess: I must be spying for another encyclopedia company. How was I to answer that? I assured her I was legit; I could send her references (obviously a bit late). She was not interested. I pleaded my case by mentioning that an editor at her company was correcting early drafts of my manuscript. She wanted to know the person's name so that they could be fired. I knew then I wasn't going to get back into that library.

I had just a few more facts to check. I told Jay Marshall of my plight. He volunteered to go to *EB*'s library, but confessed that he mainly wanted to see the expression on the librarian's face when he told her who had sent him. I found a fellow bookseller who was not quite as eager to be ejected from the hallowed halls of Encyclopaedia Britannica as Jay seemed to be. I paid this man ten dollars. We called it "combat pay." He was young, brash and brave. To be certain he obtained the correct material, he actually asked the librarian to photocopy it. "You're no better—I mean, no different—than Mr. Meyer," she said, but she must have been impressed with his bravado, for she copied the material.

The rest—the editing, typing, designing, typesetting, printing and binding of my monograph—was easy by comparison.

My 'Discoverie' of Witchcraft

REGINALD SCOT'S *The Discoverie of Witchcraft* was first published in England in 1584. "Discoverie" meant "explanation" in the language of the time, and it was Scot's aim to give a rational explanation for everything reputed to have an occult origin. This did not sit well with King James VI of Scotland (later James I of England), who was a staunch believer in the validity of witchcraft. He wrote his own book, *Daemonologie* (Edinburgh, 1597), "chiefly [to refute] the damnable opinions of Scot." To assure winning the argument, the king ordered all copies of the first edition of Scot's work to be seized and burned by the common hangman. Scholars believe this may have been a mere ceremonial act and that perhaps only one copy of Scot's work was actually burned in public.

Scot (1538–1599) had been a student at Oxford and afterward "retired" to the country, where he enjoyed gardening. He wrote his first book on the raising of hops, the important ingredient in beer, and immersed himself in what one biographer called "the study of obscure mystical authors," which resulted in his self-published *Discoverie.* Because this book covered so many subjects—witchcraft, astrology, alchemy, legerdemain and numerous related practices—it served as an important source book for the next three hundred years. William Shakespeare is said to have consulted it for witch and wizard lore when writing his plays. Today it is still considered one of the few primary resources on the study of witchcraft.

My interest in the *Discoverie* centers on the twelve chapters devoted to "the deceiptfull art of juggling," or legerdemain, commonly called *conjuring* in modern times. Scot's book is the cornerstone of every serious magic collector's library, for it is the first book in the English language to explain the techniques of the magician's art. The principles of "hiding and conveieng of balls . . . the alteration of monie . . . and the shuffeling of the cards," with examples supplied by Scot, were reproduced in nearly every magic text to appear during the next two hundred years. "Whereof some are pleasant and delectable, other some dreadful and desparate . . . all [are] but meere delusions, or counterfet actions," which is, of course, what the performance of magic is all about.

The 1584 first edition of *Discoverie* was "imprinted at London by William Brome." Although not generally considered rare, it is certainly valuable: as a 16th-

THE
Diſcovery of Witchcraft:
PROVING,
That the Compacts and Contracts of WITCHES with *Devils* and all *Infernal Spirits* or *Familiars*, are but Erroneous Novelties and Imaginary Conceptions.

Alſo diſcovering, How far their Power extendeth in Killing, Tormenting, Conſuming, or Curing the bodies of Men, Women, Children, or Animals, by Charms, Philtres, Periapts, Pentacles, Curſes, and Conjurations.

WHEREIN LIKEWISE
The Unchriſtian Practices and Inhumane Dealings of *Searchers* and *Witch-tryers* upon *Aged*, *Melancholly*, and *Superſtitious* people, in extorting Confeſſions by Terrors and Tortures and in deviſing falſe Marks and Symptoms, are notably Detected.

And the Knavery of *Juglers*, *Conjurers*, *Charmers*, *Soothſayers*, *Figure-Caſters*, *Dreamers*, *Alchymiſts* and *Philterers*; with many other things that have long lain hidden, fully Opened and Deciphered.

ALL WHICH
Are very neceſſary to be known for the undeceiving of *Judges*, *Juſtices*, and *Jurors*, before they paſs Sentence upon Poor, Miſerable and Ignorant People; who are frequenly Arraigned, Condemned, and Executed for *Witches* and *Wizzards*.

IN SIXTEEN BOOKS.

By REGINALD SCOT *Eſquire.*

Whereunto is added
An excellent Diſcourſe of the *Nature* and *Subſtance* OF
DEVILS and SPIRITS,
IN TWO BOOKS:
The *Firſt* by the aforeſaid *Author*: The *Second* now added in this *Third Edition*, as Succedaneous to the *former*, and conducing to the compleating of the *Whole Work*: With *Nine Chapters* at the beginning of the *Fifteenth Book* of the *DISCOVERY*.

LONDON:
Printed for *Andrew Clark*, and are to be ſold at Mris. *Cotes's* near the *Golden-Ball* in *Alderſgateſtreet*, 1665.

Title page of the rare second issue of the third edition of Reginald Scot's *Discoverie of Witchcraft* (London, 1665).

century book covering a breadth of magic-related and other subjects, it is always being sought by scholars and collectors in several fields. More significantly for me, this volume, printed in Gothic black-letter type, proved very troublesome, at least in the first month I owned a copy. I will soon relate why.

A second edition was printed in London in 1651. Four issues of this edition are known to exist. The first issue did not reveal a publisher's name. Considering what happened to the first edition, the publisher of the second was apparently not taking any chances about the possibility of either his books or his person being burned by the hangman.

The third edition, a tall folio with a strikingly designed title page, is the most impressive of all the editions produced. It is also the first to contain an additional seven chapters at the end of the book. This material, by an unnamed author, certainly was not written by Scot, for it deals with "the nature and substance of devils and spirits," the very existence of which Scot sought to refute in his treatise. The author of these chapters has not, to my knowledge, ever been determined, nor has the reason why they were appended to Scot's work. Two issues of this edition appeared in London under the date 1665. The second of these, "printed for Andrew Clark, and . . . to be sold at . . . Cote's near the Golden-Ball in Aldersgate Street," is cited in Raymond Toole Stott's bibliography as the scarcest edition. He notes that "only six copies are known to me." I could have shown him a seventh copy from my library.

German and French translations of Scot's *Discoverie* have been recorded, but I have never seen them. An abridged Dutch edition was published in Leyden in 1609. In 1981 I purchased a copy at an auction of "Rare Magic Books" from the library of magician-collector Milbourne Christopher. No mention was made in the catalog that the Dutch edition was published as an abridged version or that the deleted text happened to be that devoted to magic. Anyone reading the catalog would assume that in order for this edition to be included in a sale of magic books, it contained material about magic. I was thus deceived by a fellow magician. I took some comfort in the suspicion that he, too, had been deceived when buying the book, but no doubt he bought it for considerably less than I paid. However, I still own the Leyden edition and am glad I do.

No English-language editions of *Discoverie* appeared in the 18th century and only one appeared in the 19th—an 1886 reprint of the first edition (limited to 250 copies) by the London publisher Elliot Stock.

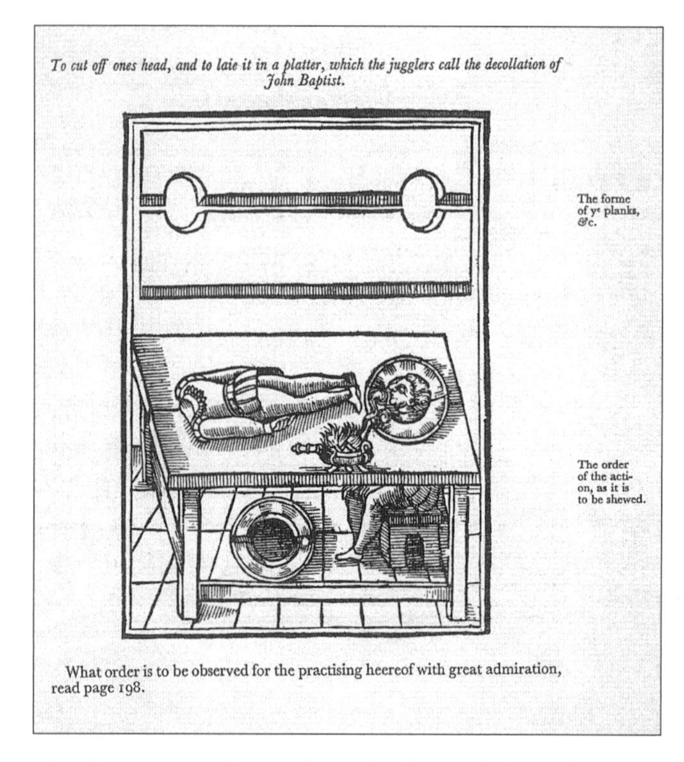

The decapitation illusion from the first and third editions of Scot's *Discoverie.*

This version possesses the most thorough explanatory notes, glossary and introduction to appear in any of the reprinted editions, and why the publisher produced so few copies remains a mystery. The extremely limited print run is my excuse for not owning a copy, but I do have a reprint issued in 1973 by EP Publishing Ltd., of Yorkshire, England.

More editions of *Discoverie* appeared during the 20th century than in Scot's own era, though several are facsimiles of earlier editions. In the late 1920s, an English publisher named John Rodker issued a series of reprints of famous texts on witchcraft, all containing introductions by the then-famous expert on the subject, the Reverend Montague Summers. A reprint of the first edition of Scot's *Discoverie* appeared as part of this series in a 1930 edition of 1,275 numbered copies, printed on watermark paper and bound in heavy boards with a leather spine. For decades, copies of this edition in new condition could be obtained on the used book market at a price comparable to remaindered books of today, but in the 1970s, as the supply finally dwindled, the price rose. A good copy now commands several hundred dollars.

Another series that included Scot's book was the Centaur Classics, issued by London's Centaur Press and encompassing works of English poetry, biography

No. 1281. **The Knife for Cutting off any Person's Nose.**—An ordinary table knife is given for examination. The performer then takes it, and gashes it into his nose, as shown in the drawing, and leaves it there for a short time, causing a thrill of horror to run through the audience, and yet upon being implored to remove it, he does so, and there is not the slightest scar or wound, whilst the knife may be once more examined.

Price 3/- *Post free* 3/3. *With full directions.*

An "apparatus to cut your nose asunder" first appeared in Scot's *Discoverie.* Over two hundred years later, this version was offered in Hamley Brothers' *Illustrated Catalogue of Conjuring Tricks* (London, 1896).

and history, and early translations of Greek literature. *Discoverie,* with a scholarly introduction by Hugh Ross Williamson, was published in 1964.

Perhaps the oddest edition ever to appear was an "abridged replica" of the first edition, privately printed in 1954 by John McArdle, an amateur magician and obvious eccentric. In addition to reproductions of title pages of earlier editions, a Scot family tree, and photographs of Scot's hometown church and tomb, McArdle's introduction includes a photograph of himself dressed as "Reginald Scot, Esquire." With a copy of the first edition of *Discoverie* tucked under his arm and costumed in a feathered cap, starched accordion collar and fake beard, McArdle looks more like a jester than an author. His edition, which thankfully consisted of only fifty copies, was remaindered for a dollar each, but if a copy can be found these days, it is likely to cost over six hundred dollars.

Reprints of Rodker's edition of Scot continue to appear. In the 1990s a small press publisher in Washington, D.C., which caters to collectors of magic books, offered a hardcover version for $40 (but later reduced the price) and specially bound and numbered copies for $80. Dover Publications, known for its excellent facsimiles printed on acid-free paper and bound in sturdy paper covers, supplied the same version for $11.95.

Why do I mention all these editions? Because I sought them all. But of them all, my acquisition of the first edition remains the most memorable because of the events surrounding its purchase.

My father and I bought wonderful books for several decades from a dealer on the outskirts of London named George W. Walford. After his retirement, his firm continued under his name, selling mostly illustrated and natural history books. From Mr. Walford I had already acquired two variants of the third edition of Scot's *Discoverie* and nearly a shelf of other English and continental conjuring books published in the 18th century. I knew he had a copy of Scot in a first edition, for it had been offered in at least three of his catalogs prior to my arrival in London in the fall of 1974. I had long wanted one, but the price of 250 pounds, equivalent to $500 at that time, was more than I had ever paid for a book and more than I thought I could afford. Still, I phoned him. He warned me that he had only a warehouse, not a store. Everything offered was listed in his catalogs, yet if I wanted to come and "browse in the dark," I was welcome to.

The ride to his neighborhood took nearly an hour on the Underground and, despite his directions, I became lost as soon as I set out on foot. It was a poor workingman's suburb, with long streets of rundown houses and not a retail shop in sight. Finally I ventured into a pub to ask directions. I may have been the first American to step in since World War II, for everyone stopped drinking or playing darts to stare at me. I was quickly given directions and again set on my way.

Mr. Walford had not been kidding: the books were not arranged for viewing and the light was so dim I was amazed he hadn't gone blind. (He did wear exceptionally thick-lensed glasses.) I knew immediately that there was nothing I could find without his help or one

Not much to look at: George Walford's warehouse, London, circa 1970.

of his catalogs in hand. I asked if he had any conjuring books, such as I had bought from him before—and did he still have the Scot's *Discoverie* listed in his last several catalogs?

Indeed he did. He brought it out and laid it in my hands. I was sold the minute I held it. I say "*I* was sold" rather than "the book was sold" because as much as I wanted this first edition of Scot, as I told Mr. Walford, I didn't have enough money with me to actually buy it. Would he hold it for me until I returned to America and could send for it?

"Oh, just take it along and I'll send a bill." His nonchalance surprised me, no doubt because I felt so uncomfortable just holding the book. I remember nodding numbly and wondering, as he wrapped it, how I would manage to get it safely back home—this oldest and most expensive book I had ever owned.

I kept it with me wherever I went in London but it wasn't until I reached the States that my first nerve-racking experience occurred. As is the standard practice, before landing I filled out the customs form, expecting that an old book, especially one nearly four hundred years old at that time, would require a ransom in custom duties. The agent, a young woman with an intense curiosity, looked at my declaration form and asked to see the book. I unwrapped it for her. She took it from me. My heart stopped. A stranger was holding, then opening, then leafing through my Scot. Then she walked away with it. I watched her walk around the room showing off the book to other agents. They wanted to hold it, too. Several did just that. I was in agony. Finally, she returned and handed it back, expressing her amazement that books could last for nearly four hundred years. I wanted to say, "Not if they're handled by custom agents." Instead I asked her, probably with perspiration dotting my forehead, how much in custom fees I owed.

"Oh, nothing," she said; "there's no duty on old books."

Several months later I happened to be in the home of a well-known collector of magic books who, to put it politely, was a braggart. His conversation usually focused on himself and, if he was talking about books, it was about *his* books. As we viewed his collection, I began to grow tired of his triumphant tone of voice, as if he alone could own such fine books. When he came to his copy of the first edition of Scot's *Discoverie of Witchcraft,* he proudly said, "This book cost me five hundred dollars twenty years ago."

"Really?" I said, equally proud and no less boastful. "I paid five hundred dollars for mine about three months ago."

"Oh, yours," he said without an instant of hesitation, "must be a bastard copy."

"A what?"

"A bastard copy. Made up of parts from several defective copies. Bound as one."

I felt again those deadly droplets of perspiration pop out on my forehead. Had I been younger I might have cried. Had I been older I might have had a stroke. His words struck me to the heart. He had hurt me and hurt me badly, which is probably what I deserved for trying to crow in *his* library. If I wanted to crow about my books, I should have waited until someone visited *my* library.

He did not, in fact, know anything about my Scot, and should not have made such a pronouncement about it. Certainly he did not intend to ruin my day and never realized he had. He talked blithely on about his other treasures, but my only thought and interest from that moment on was to return home to confirm or disallow his conviction. I spent a sleepless, miserable night at his home and was never more thankful than when I left.

On my arrival home I fearfully (and carefully) checked my copy of Scot and afterwards showed it to a bookseller friend who routinely handled books of Scot's vintage. He assured me my copy was whole and one.

Several weeks later, in Sotheby's London auction rooms, a copy of the first edition of Scot's *Discoverie of Witchcraft* sold for 2,500 pounds, or $5,000. The price for this book has not much varied from that figure to this day. My copy at 250 pounds was a bargain indeed. So whatever that grandiose collector had to say, I could easily forgive him his mistake. But as you see, I can never forget it.

CONJURORS

Several Landmarks and an Icon

LOVE AFFAIRS ABOUND in the world of magic. Close-up magicians love card tricks. Stage magicians love illusions. Amateurs love the apparatus for parlor tricks even though they seldom have a parlor in which to perform them. Collectors love magicians of the past and all the artifacts—from fake thumbtips to posters the size of a barn—associated with magic history. Nearly all magicians of note—Houdini and Blackstone come easily to mind—are loved long after their deaths by magicians still living. And if you want to become immortal, a friend used to say, write a magic book. Many are embraced as bibles.

My first love in magic was a building. It was slightly larger than a newsstand, with a front window framed by dark blue mirrored glass. Sitting in a corner of an otherwise empty block on a main thoroughfare, it was clearly used originally as an office for a car lot, but in my youth it was Wayne's Trick Shop. I couldn't ride into town without watching for it, hoping my Dad would stop.

Wayne was a tall (to a ten-year-old), middle-aged man with a gravelly voice who built a following of boy magicians from cities around Northwest Indiana. His shop, which I cannot recall having an exterior sign and seemed to be open only a few days a week, could not accommodate more than half a dozen customers at a time. Standing shoulder to shoulder with others in the narrow space between the window and the counters full of jokes and tricks, one had to maneuver back and forth in order to see everything.

Most of Wayne's magic wares were the standard marketed effects available in novelty shops or the toy section of large department stores. A few stage-size props were also on display. Wayne was not always a willing demonstrator of magic. He might suggest that you buy a trick and take it home to find out for yourself what it was all about. Once the secret was known, of course, it could not be returned for a refund if you didn't like it.

To accommodate the growing number of boy magicians in the area, Wayne formed a club which held its monthly meetings in a VFW hall. The format was simple. Members would perform tricks they had bought at Wayne's, then Wayne would perform a new trick and take orders for it. Ascending the stage, a must-do at each meeting, was a stomach-churning challenge for me, but it actually didn't matter how good or bad I was. There wasn't much concerted effort to entertain. You merely demonstrated what you had taught yourself at home and, as many of the tricks were of the pocket variety, they could barely be seen by anyone beyond the first row.

I fell out of love with Wayne's Trick Shop after the incident of the Die Box. This was a dandy trick which Wayne performed one evening at the VFW. A box—a large box even in his hefty hands—was shown with two doors on the front. The doors were opened to expose two chambers with a dividing wall in between. A large block of wood painted with white dots to resemble a single die was taken out of an upturned hat sitting on a nearby table. The die was placed within a chamber of the box and the door closed. As Wayne explained that he was about to vanish the die, he slightly tipped the box and everyone could hear the die slide into the adjoining chamber. He opened the door and proclaimed that the die had vanished. But the die was now in the other chamber! No, said Wayne, tipping the box the other way, which revealed the sound of the die sliding back into the first chamber. He opened the door to the second chamber and showed it empty. This back-and-forth foolery went on for a while and in the end both doors were opened to show the die had indeed vanished. Wayne picked it out of the upturned hat from which he had originally taken it. Then he took orders for this magnificent trick.

I can still see Wayne's Die Box: larger than my grandfather's humidor and of a similarly dark stained wood with a high-gloss varnish. The doors on the front were trimmed with bright brass fittings. It was a splendid piece of apparatus and Wayne would order it for only fifteen dollars.

Who in that bunch of boys carried fifteen dollars in his wallet? We all went home that night determined to somehow collect the money and anxiously await the first chance to return to Wayne's shop to pay him. After the money was paid, weeks went by. At the next monthly meeting of the magic club, we were eager to receive our Die Boxes, but they weren't there. They had not come in yet, Wayne announced. The wait became worse than buying something from Johnson Smith Company's catalog of nine thousand novelties. At least with Johnson Smith you could anticipate receiving your package within two weeks, and every day you checked the mailbox with high anticipation (and then deflation) until your order arrived. But calling Wayne or stopping by his shop to inquire about the Die Box never brought a response beyond "Nope"—nothing so much as a comforting "It'll be here soon."

After several months my enthusiasm finally evaporated, as it must have for other boys, and even hope began to fade. My father suggested that I ask for my money back.

When my Die Box finally arrived, it was nothing like the one Wayne had demonstrated. The wood, painted black with a white stenciled design of a dragon on each door, looked exotic and mysterious enough, but it lacked the richness of Wayne's varnished version. Instead of heavy brass fittings, the doors were attached by painted hinges. Most noticeable of all, my Die Box was less than half the size of Wayne's. He had shown a stage illusion and I was receiving a parlor trick. Perhaps the months that passed were meant to cloud the memory of his Die Box. I accepted my version (which was, after all, more my size) and I used it, but I was never fully comfortable with Wayne again. I soon left his club and put his trick shop behind me.

By then I had begun my almost weekly trips to Chicago by commuter train with my grandmother Grace or by car with my parents. They went to shop and I tagged along, hoping for and usually finding an opportunity to visit a magic shop. My favorites were Ireland Magic Company and National Magic, although The Treasure Chest, an always crowded novelty and trick emporium on Randolph Street, was worth stopping by just to glimpse its towering overhead sign. Probably weighing a ton or more, it consisted of multi-dozens of long neon bulbs which began at the store's entrance and reached skyward above the roof. In retrospect, the sign was the best part of the place, for I never felt comfortable among The Treasure Chest crowd. They were boys about my age but from rougher backgrounds, elbowing each other out of the way in order to buy a "fly in the ice cube" gag or fake vomit. The clerks behind the counter were often as harried as the servers at our local ice cream shop.

Also on Randolph Street was the Woods Theatre building where, for a few years, Clarke "The Senator" Crandall had a shop, although it seemed to be more of a hangout than a business. Crandall, a close-up magician with a wire-thin waxed mustache, was both funny and sarcastic, often at the same instant. (His philosophy about magic books, as expressed in an inscription to the card conjuror Rufus Steele, was "It's not what you do—it's not the way you do it—it's the way you write it that counts.") His store was even smaller than Wayne's and it wasn't unusual to have to stand in the doorway if enough customers had converged in front of his single counter. Strewn around, rather than displayed, were small effects, parts of tricks, gimmicks and accumulations of this-and-that.

Crandall did sell magic, digging out something to demonstrate just to be doing something. He was equally content to merely trade gossip with his cronies, one or more of whom were always there. (Jay Marshall admits to taking friends to Crandall's for "the laughs," which were more frequent there than at his wife's shop.) Crandall always attracted professional magicians who were performing in Chicago. I remember once standing next to Del Ray, a star of magic at the time, who was engaged at The Empire Room of The Palmer House. The sight which most impressed me in Crandall's was a framed poster of stage illusionist Howard Thurston (1869–1936) performing the vanishing Whippet car. Where Crandall had obtained it, I never learned. He was not a man known for his interest in illusions or in magic's past.

I could not—and still cannot—enter the Palmer House Hotel without thinking of the National Magic Company. In its heyday in the 1940s it must have been a thriving enterprise. The "studio—the largest and finest in the world," as described and depicted in a photo in their mail-order catalog no. 3, consisted of two rows of floor- and wall-display counters running the length of the room, with a small stage centered between them. Four clerks were attending to three customers when the photo was taken.

The studio was on the third floor of the hotel, in a dim and silent corridor, reminiscent to me of moody thrillers of the thirties which I watched on late-night TV. It was seldom open in those days, the early 1960s, and glancing through the window into the dark interior only added to the aura of mystery. To gain entrance you had to go to the Palmer House Gift Shop in the street-level arcade. There you waited until Vic Torsberg or his brother Chuck had time to open the magic shop. They accompanied you back upstairs, unlocked the door, turned on the lights, and then waited for you.

Much of what I bought there was pocket magic, but well made, either of sleek plastic or polished wood. The appearance of the apparatus was often better than the trick. The "Miracle Ball Thru Glass" was one of these. A shallow walnut casket, which lay neatly in the palm of one's hand, had a hole drilled through the lid and down through the bottom half which cradled a loose piece of glass. The box was opened, the glass and a marble (the "miracle ball") sitting on top of it were removed, and the box was offered for inspection. Everything seemed solid, although the corners on one side of the box did not fit quite as tightly together as those on the other. After the glass was replaced, the lid was closed and secured with a small metal hasp which

No. M12 **MIRACLE BALL THRU GLASS**

A beautifully made walnut box 4¼ inches long, 2⅝ inches wide and ¾ inch deep, is given for examination and attention called to the holes in top and bottom, also the removable glass plate which fits snugly inside.

A spectator is requested to place the glass in the box and fasten the clasp.

A glass marble is next given for examination and is placed by the spectator in the hole of the cover. The glass of course prevents the marble from falling thru.

Performer holds the box in front of him when suddenly to the amazement of everyone, the ball is seen to slowly sink thru the box and glass and fall out the bottom.

Everything—Box, Glass and Marble is again given for inspection. A wonderful pocket trick that will fool the wisest. We draw particular attention to the fine precision workmanship of our Box.

N.M.C.

Price, **$3.00**....................Postpaid, **$3.10**

Catalog illustration for National Magic Company's "Miracle Ball Thru Glass," showing its length to be nearly shoulder-to-shoulder. However, the actual apparatus does not cover the palm of a man's hand.

fit over a decorative knob jutting from one end of the bottom section of the box. The marble was placed in the top hole of the box and the magic began. With the box held at the spectator's eye level, the marble slowly sank out of sight, into the box, through it and out the bottom hole. The box was reopened and offered for inspection again. The glass was still in place—undamaged. Solid through solid!

The secret was to pull on that little knob sticking through the hasp without being detected. This released the bottom panel of the box from three of the sides which framed it. As the bottom was slowly inched toward you (yet out of view of the spectator), the marble descended. However, the movable part of the box did not slide as smoothly as a drawer being pulled out of a dresser, and getting it back in place and the knob tucked in again was always the panic part of the trick. One diversion was to do the trick away from a carpeted area, for this had the spectator scrambling to pick up the fallen marble as it rolled around while you were struggling to reseat the bottom of the box. Performing the trick over concrete was not a good idea, however, as the pane of glass remained intact but the marble might not. "Miracle Ball Thru Glass" was a clever concept and a handsome little piece of apparatus, but hardly a miracle.

National Magic Company fascinated me. Its quiet, out-of-the-way location, where no other customers appeared while I was there, gave me the sense that it was a sanctuary for magic, rather than a store selling it. The apparatus on display didn't need to be performed to have meaning; behind glass, with their mysteries intact, they seemed already to have a history and become artifacts. Forty years later some of those tricks I gazed upon are now, no doubt, treasured in private collections.

Above the door hung a portrait of the stage magician Harry Blackstone, Senior (1885–1965). It was a good likeness, painted in mid-life when he personified the perfect "look" of a magician: the wild white hair, the heavy eyebrows, the captivating smile. You couldn't help noticing it when you left the store. I think I asked more than once who had painted it, but no one knew. I was told it belonged to Jim Sherman, the absentee owner of National Magic, who lived in California. When Sherman closed the business in the early 1970s, the display counters went to Jay and Frances Marshall's shop, Magic, Inc., but I never learned what happened to Blackstone's portrait.

Another wonderland was Ed Miller's Museum of Magic. I suspect the name was dreamed up for the exhibitions of posters and photos from Miller's collection which were mounted at several magic conventions in the 1950s. The covers of the souvenir brochures for these occasions displayed a picture of Miller as a tight-lipped man with a steely gaze. This was certainly Ed Miller as I remember him. Printed in black-and-white, the brochures did not do justice to the marvelous four-color lithographs of magicians on display.

You couldn't call Miller's place a museum or a magic store (it was a workshop), but if you managed to find it and start up a conversation with its laconic owner, there was a possibility that he might part with something you came across in the clutter. Knowing of my interest in the history of magic, Frances Marshall suggested I go there.

In the summer of 1961 Miller was located in four rooms of a second-floor walkup above a cafeteria at 436 North Clark Street, just across the river from Chicago's Loop. A faded paper tag announcing "MAGIC" was taped on the window of the old building's weathered door. Opening it, you faced a flight of stairs and could hear a buzzer sound above. As you passed through another set of doors halfway up, a bell warned of your arrival. "The walls of the rooms," I wrote in my journal after my first visit, "are covered with posters, handbills and ad material of magicians of the past and present." I couldn't adequately describe what an amazing and disorganized place I happened on when I reached the top of those stairs.

In his younger years Miller had been a professional magician and clown (still hard for me to believe, considering his retiring manner), but by the time I met him he was constructing apparatus for performers and other dealers. Throughout his life he acquired everything he could lay his hands on relating to magicians of the past and those he met or had known. He may have been the greatest unsung magic collector of his time. Like Houdini a generation before him, Miller was collecting when the value of things magical was in terms of nostalgia, not dollars. Many of the rare photographs and autographed letters of magic's earlier luminaries, which are now neatly matted and fancily framed and hanging in the dens of magic aficionados, came from Ed Miller's hoard. In his shop the letters, photos, business cards, handbills and other ephemera were pasted on large boards or filled cardboard boxes. Two of the most renowned magic poster collections of our day incorporate what Ed Miller had owned. Posters were stacked by the hundreds in packing cases in his shop. They shared space with his machinery and materials for making props.

Facing Miller that first time, I was a seventeen-year-old nobody who, like so many others who had wandered in, was there to waste his time. I can't say he ever warmed to me (did he to anyone?), yet when he realized I was more than just curious and in fact had a measure of knowledge about magic's past, he showed me around. After several visits I found the courage to ask him if he had anything he would be willing to sell me. We were standing by a wooden box filled with one-sheet lithographs. The poster on top was of George Shade performing a large production box illusion—not a very colorful, interesting or exciting litho, but it probably typified Shade's career. Would I want one of these, Miller asked. It was one of several duplicates and the price was right. Five dollars. All these many years later, I can't help wondering what I would have carried home that day if we had been standing by a box full of Houdini posters.

Frances Marshall did me another favor that summer. She sent me to see Theo Bamberg. A revered icon in magic, he was eighty-six years old when I met him. As the fifth or possibly the sixth generation of a family line of Dutch magicians, he was the descendant of court conjurors. In the guise of "Okito," an Oriental, Bamberg had played throughout Europe in the best variety houses. He sold his act at the height of success, then endeavored to establish a magic business in New York; later he toured with illusionist Howard Thurston and teamed up with the mentalist Zancig, but finally hit bottom and attempted suicide. He eventually moved to South America, recast his Okito act and again became a headliner in theatres in South America and Europe in the 1920s and '30s. He was known for his artistry as a performer and for his craftsmanship in the invention and building of fine apparatus.

But as often happens in show business, in old age he was alone and living a spartan life in a second-rate hotel in Chicago.

A record of Okito's life's work was written by Bamberg in collaboration with Robert Parrish. Titled *Okito on Magic,* it was published in Chicago in 1952 and is now considered a classic. My father bought my copy from Frances Marshall in December 1957 and gave it to me for Christmas, my fourteenth birthday. After I read the book, I wanted to become an Oriental magician. I can be forgiven this conceit because of my age. Others dressing in kimonos and fixing up their eyebrows will have to find their own excuses for failing to recreate the exotic magic of Okito. My father indulged my fantasy by taking me to Toguri Trading Company in Chicago, where I was fitted with a cotton kimono, toe-split socks and bamboo sandals by the niece of the owner. This lady, a Japanese-American, had gone by the name of Tokyo Rose during World War II. In radio broadcasts to Allied troops taking back the Pacific islands during the later years of the war, she urged them to surrender—a treasonable act. She was remanded to her family by some decree of our government and here she was, outfitting me for my Oriental magic act which never came to be.

Before setting off to see Okito that summer day in

Theodore "Okito" Bamberg (1875–1963). When he was photographed in his magnificent Oriental stage costume, there wasn't much room left for an autograph.

1961, I asked Frances what I might take him as a gift. She suggested dates. I bought a package at the Stop and Shop Store on Randolph Street and carried it with my copy of *Okito on Magic.* Nervousness nearly derailed my mission, but after walking around the same block several times, I found the courage to enter the lobby of The Wacker Hotel and take the elevator up. The dates made it easy after that. Okito was delighted the moment I handed them to him, while still standing in the doorway. We sat down in his little room which, I recall, contained little more than a bed, dresser, chair and his wardrobe trunk. He sat on his bed and offered me the chair. It was the first day of August, hot and humid, and there was no fan or air conditioner in the room. We talked more about me than about magic. He urged me to continue my education and repeated this later in a letter, sent along with an inscribed copy of a book for which he had written an introduction. No doubt "continue your education" was his admonition to all young magicians, based on his experiences in life. It was as if he were saying, "Don't take up magic as a livelihood." Our meeting that day was short, for he was expecting someone to whom he was giving lessons in sleight of hand. He signed my copy of his book: "To David Meyer, in kind remembrance of Okito."

What significance did our meeting have? In any

ordinary sense, none. I never saw him again. I did not (until now) write anything about him or collect his beautifully made props or perform any of his signature tricks. But my admiration for him was cemented by that meeting and has never dulled since.

Twenty-seven years later, when the autobiography of his son David Bamberg was passing around in manuscript form and came my way, I published it. I believed it to be one of the most interesting and honest accounts of the life of a traveling showman, far surpassing almost everything written by or about any other magician of that time. It also happened to include much about his father, Okito. David Bamberg's *Illusion Show* was the fifth book I published on the subject of magic and more have appeared since. I guess I did not follow Okito's advice after all.

A Glimpse of Martin Sunshine

THIS IS ABOUT A SCRAPBOOK and a summer's day.

In the early 1990s I purchased a roomful of magic books in Toledo, Ohio. They had once been the inventory of The Tigner Magic Supply Company, a sideline business of a college professor who founded and edited *The Journal of Magic History,* the only scholarly publication of its kind. Although *JMH* lasted for only six issues, it helped to prove that magic as a performing art was a viable part of theatre history and worthy of study.

Among the Tigner items I acquired was a blue binder labeled "Martin Sunshine." In it are programs, booking brochures, original advertising art, letters of agreement, photographs and news clippings. They are from various periods of Martin Sunshine's career as a stage mentalist in partnership with his wife, Betty Ann Mortonson, and also for his solo act as Kismet the magician.

The earliest piece is a program for the annual outing of the Sons of Delaware of Philadelphia, an organization of University of Delaware alumni, dated May

The Sunshines as represented by The White Entertainment Bureau of New York, Inc. (c. 1930).

17, 1924. The next-to-closing act was Sunshine & Sunshine's "Can Such Things Be?"

Three pages from *The New Yorker* magazine's weekly "Goings On About Town" sections for the month of April 1930 list the couple's appearance at The County Fair in Greenwich Village. A clipping from *The Sphinx* for June 1932 contains an editorial which notes that "the Sunshines work so fast with their mindreading that at the beginning a number of people felt that it must be a series of pre-arrangements. A lady near me felt quite certain that Martin used only his own confederates, but when he finally got to her and asked for her name, Betty said 'Stella' so rapidly, it sounded like an echo."

A copy of "Invitational Travel Orders" from the Department of the Army, dated 26 March 1952, includes the names of Sunshine and nine other performers. They were to report "for movement by military aircraft to Burtonwood, England; thence to North Africa; Trieste [Italy]; France; Heidelberg, Germany; Azores Islands; Northeast Air Command, Newfoundland, and to other such places within these commands . . . for the purpose of entertaining military personnel."

A photocopy of the obit page from *Genii, The Conjurors' Magazine* for October 1978 was obviously added by Tigner. It carries a brief notice of the death of Martin Sunshine on August 9th in Rhinelander, Wisconsin.

One of the last items in the binder is a letter dated August 1980 from Tigner to a man in Saugus, California. Tigner wanted to know where the man had found Martin Sunshine's photos and clippings—and were there more?

Accompanying the scrapbook was an audiocassette of Robert and Elaine Lund, proprietors of the American Museum of Magic, talking with Martin Sunshine on the day the Lunds purchased from him several pieces of equipment once owned by Harry Houdini.

As with most conversations, theirs went in one direction, then another, and often turned back to an earlier topic. It is clear, however, that Bob Lund was intent on learning about Martin Sunshine's life and career, and on saving this brief oral history. The following transcript—although abbreviated, occasionally rearranged and with some editorial intrusion—is what was said on that summer's day. Why this tape belongs with Martin Sunshine's scrapbook will become apparent at the end.

Robert Lund is identified by his initials (RL), as are Elaine Lund (EL) and Martin Sunshine (MS).

RL Monday, August twenty-third, 1976. I'm in Three Lakes, Wisconsin.

MS That's right!

RL With Marty Sunshine. We are standing in the front yard of his home. We have here Houdini's milk can and the three giant pails he used [for filling it].

MS I'm also known as Kismet.

RL Ah, yes. You said you knew both Houdini and [his brother] Hardeen.

MS I worked with Hardeen on shows and I was supposed to open the Houdini theatre in Fort Worth, Texas, years ago and Hardeen was going to run it. It was [to be] called the House of Houdini but we were delayed. [Theatrical producer] Billy Rose was building it.

RL Do you remember the year that was?

MS It was around 1932. Hardeen and Houdini's assistant—what was his name?

RL Collins. Jimmy Collins.

MS Yeah, Jimmy Collins, Hardeen and I were the first ones down there, but the place wasn't ready and we came back to New York. In the meantime, I got a job in the West Indies at a nightclub and I couldn't go ahead with the plan with Hardeen. So he got someone else to take my place.

RL You know, I saw your ad for the Milk Can and pails in *Tops* magazine years ago and I figured they had been sold so I never got in touch with you. . . . Then I got a letter from Chrystal Dunninger, a good friend of mine, and she said, "You ought to get in touch with Marty Sunshine. He's still got that Houdini stuff; it would be great for your magic museum."

MS I know Chrystal and Joe Dunninger* very well.

RL Tell me how you happened to come to Three Lakes, Wisconsin.

*Joseph Dunninger (1892–1975), a magician and mentalist, wrote many books on both subjects. He hosted radio and TV shows as a mentalist in the 1940s and '50s.

MS I used to work here for the Music Corporation of America.

RL Working out of Chicago?

MS Right. [They had] the Marnie Showboat, which opened in 1940. I was supposed to be here [performing in the nightclub] for two weeks and I stayed nine weeks until they closed. I came back, year after year, for thirty-one years.

RL What do you do with yourself the rest of the time, when you're not here? Do you travel?

MS When I leave here I immediately go to California. I stay there at least until New Year's and after that I go to Florida. I work the cruises down there. Then around April I go up to New York to visit my nieces and nephews and I come back here in May.

RL Do you have any children?

MS No. No children.

RL How long have you been a magician?

MS Professional and amateur? Since 1911.

RL And what started you in magic?

MS I was walking home and just happened to pass a magic shop on Eighth Avenue [in New York City]. I bought a trick there and fooled the kids and felt so proud about it. I was able to fool them! So I kept on buying more tricks.

RL Where were you born? Were you born in New York City?

MS I was born in Harrisburg, Pennsylvania.

RL What was the transition from a boy magician into a professional? Did you just keep at it and gradually became a professional?

MS That's right.

RL Do you feel any regrets at letting this [Houdini equipment] go? You've had it so many years.

MS Well, I'll tell you. I've had antique dealers offer me more for these [brass pails] than for anything else.

RL And you bought this from Hardeen?

MS The reason I bought it from the Hardeen estate was to keep it out of the hands of amateurs who might expose it.

RL Well, it will never be exposed in my possession. I'm going to really make a feature exhibit out of it and build a nice display stand for it.

MS I'll give you the trunk, too. The Overboard Packing Case. That's here, too.

RL You said you knew Houdini. Where did you meet Houdini?

MS Oh, I met him several times. I was working Pottstown, Pennsylvania. I was entertaining at the Rotary Club there and Houdini was at the Orpheum

Theatre—I think it was the Orpheum Theatre—and when I got through with my show, I went [to see his]. He was exposing the spirit mediums. He used to have a question-and-answer thing and I knew one of his favorite questions and I sat in the back and said, "How about so-and-so?" He loved that. I was registered at the same hotel with him and we got talking and sat up until about three or four o'clock in the morning.

He had detectives investigating different spiritualists. [When I arrived at his room] he was talking on the telephone with one of these investigators and said, "Now look. Answer what I'm asking you. You're spending my time and money. If I ask you a question, just answer that question. Never mind something else." You know, he was a tough little guy. He was tough.

RL What kind of fellow was Hardeen?

MS He wasn't as smooth as Houdini. I saw Hardeen once in a theatre. He said to me, "Sunshine, come on down and catch my show at the Twenty-third Street Theatre." I'm sure it was the Twenty-third Street Theatre in New York, and I went down to see him and went backstage after that. He wasn't the showman, nowhere near the showman that Houdini was. So he said, "What do you think of the show?" and I said, "Well, look." We used to call him Dash, that was his nickname. I said, "Dash, look outside [the theatre].

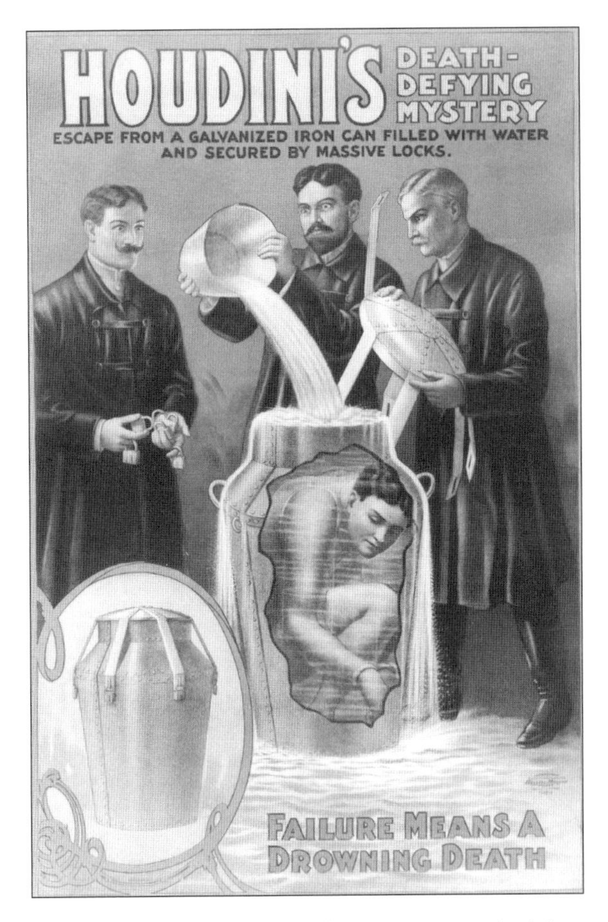

Poster for Houdini's famous Milk Can Escape, which he performed in music halls and variety theatres throughout Europe during the period 1905–1910. (Poster courtesy of Tad Ware.)

Robert Lund with the Houdini Milk Can Escape display in his American Museum of Magic. (Photo by David Odette.)

You got 'Brother of Houdini' and the fact that you inherited all his tricks [in all your advertising outside]. Now, Harry was known for the overboard packing case, the upside-down straitjacket escape—this, that and the other—but you're doing a lot of *other* junk. Why don't you *do* the tricks that you inherited from your brother . . . ?" I saw him a couple of days later and he said, "My manager told me to add more stuff to the show. . . ." Did you see Houdini's show?

RL No.

MS Well, he used to throw a clock over there and it would disappear and come down on a string. [Al Baker* and] I had a set of these clocks and we advertised it in *The Sphinx.* Hardeen heard about it and he wrote me a letter. He wrote, "I heard you're peddling the Houdini Clock Trick" or whatever it was. He was mad as hell when he wrote me and I wrote back a letter and said, "Look, we're not peddlers, we're a legitimate business. We bought this and it's for sale and if you think it ought to be off the market and you want

*Al Baker (1874–1951) performed a ventriloquism and magic act in vaudeville and Chautauqua. One of the most prominent and beloved magicians of his time, he became Dean of the Society of American Magicians in 1938. His books *Magical Ways and Means* (1941), *Mental Magic* (1949) and *Pet Secrets* (1951) are still read and valued.

to buy it, the price is so much." And that's the last I heard from him.

RL You were in business with Al Baker at one time.

MS That's right. We had the Broadway Magic Shop at 1472 Broadway [in New York City].

RL How long did you have that business?

MS About three or four years, I think.

RL What kind of guy was Al Baker?

MS The most honest man in the world. We got along very well.

RL Did you make any money in that magic shop?

MS We made it. As I said before, Al was a very honest man. But he gave it away. I'll give you an example of what would happen. One day we got an order for some trick, I forget [what it was]. It sold for a dollar and Al said to some kid, "Here, I'll give you a quarter if you'll mail this for us." The item cost us sixty cents. It cost us fifteen cents to mail and he gave the kid a quarter—so we didn't make a penny on it. That's the kind of guy he was.

RL Did you ever hear any stories about Houdini and Dunninger together?

MS No. I know Chrystal and Joe very well. I've known them for years. I have the last book he wrote [*Dunninger's Secrets,* written in 1974 with Walter B. Gibson]. He sent me one autographed. He died that same year. I used to go round to his home when he was on Cauldwell Avenue [in New York]. His mother would get up and makc us a cup of coffee or get us a bottle of beer and a sandwich. I knew Joe for many years. He wanted me to teach Chrystal the act I was doing with my ex-wife, Betty Ann. Joe and [his friend] Dave Lustig* would ride around in Joe's car and my wife and I would be in the back. Joe and Dave would try to stump us.

RL Was it an oral code [that you and your wife had worked up for your mental act]?

MS Yes, it was my own. It took me fourteen years to perfect it. We could call out first and last names. Some guy in Annapolis wanted to buy [the act]. I said, "Fifteen hundred dollars." He said, "Would you start me on installments?" I said, "No."

EL How did you happen to call yourself Kismet?

MS Well, you see, years ago, when we worked in vaudeville, if you were a dancer, the rest of your life you were known as a dancer. Now, if suddenly you discovered you had a wonderful voice, [the booking agents] couldn't see you as a singer. They knew you [only] as a dancer. They knew us as a mental act, Betty

*David Lustig (1893–1977) performed professionally as "La Vellma" the mentalist.

and Martin Sunshine. So I changed the name so I could get work. I called myself Kismet. It means "destiny, fate." The origin is Persian.

I worked a show once [as the Sunshines and returned as Kismet, and my agent said to the theatre manager], "Do you know this fellow Kismet?" And he said, "I never saw him before." I was a different act, so they wanted to see me.

RL How would you describe the act you do today?

MS Comedy magic.

RL Who's the best magician you ever saw?

MS They were all the best—the one that was working.

RL Would you say you've had a full life and magic's been kind to you? Sum it up for me.

MS Well, if I had to do it over again, I'd do it over again. [Even] overseas to entertain the Armed Forces [during World War II]. I was in the South Pacific with two other fellows. I stayed there nine months. [On] June 16, 1943, I was doing one of my tricks and we got an alert. We had to go to our foxholes. The Japanese came over us and the American boys brought down 125 Japanese planes that day. I'll never forget that day. I was on that island for a month. We slept in tents and then when I got through there, I went up to the Aleutian [Islands]. We slept in tents [when it was] sixty be-

Martin Sunshine as "Kismet the Magician" performing for "the brass"—a two-star general and a colonel—while touring the Pacific with the U.S.O. during World War II.

low zero, and I think, I'm almost sure, I was the first magician to work U.S.O. shows [up there]. They didn't want magicians, but the man who booked me there said, "I want to show them they don't know what they're talking about." After I got on they started to advertise for magicians.

Well, I'll tell you something. If I find it, I'll send you [a clipping from one of those] New York City "official rags." . . . They sent up a regular—you know, an interviewer—to interview us when I was doing the mindreading act. The *New York World-Telegram* carried a whole column and *The New York Evening Post* did a double column.

EL You mean you have a scrapbook with these things?

MS I've got seventeen scrapbooks!

EL You do!

MS Oh boy, you should see the stuff in those scrapbooks. You should see some of the pictures I got in the South Pacific when I was there. I had to wear a uniform. In uniform I got some beautiful, good pictures from down there. Yep.

THE TAPE ENDS HERE, on the mention of scrapbooks.

What happened to those seventeen scrapbooks? I know the fate of only one. In 1980 Tigner placed an ad in a newspaper for collectors buying and selling antiques. He advertised his interest in obtaining anything on magic and used the name "The Friends of Magic History" with his address. The ad brought a response he never expected: a parcel from a man in California containing, in Tigner's words, "four decades of memorabilia" collected by Martin Sunshine. The man was not asking for payment; he was simply sending Martin Sunshine's photos and clippings to "The Friends of Magic History" for safekeeping. Tigner wrote back expressing his surprise and delight and, "dying of curiosity," asked for "further enlightenment." How did these materials come into the man's possession? Tigner had hopes he was corresponding with someone who had been in show business himself and had known Martin Sunshine when he was a stage mentalist and performed as Kismet. But the answer was a sad one.

"I don't know anything else about Mr. Sunshine," the man replied. He had found everything in a trash barrel.

Portrait of a Popularizer

OF ALL THE "CLASSIC" 20th-century textbooks on magic in the English language, John Northern Hilliard's 1,030-page *Greater Magic* and the multi-volumed *Tarbell Course* come most easily to magicians' minds. There are others, of course, and one of these goes by the unimpressive title of *The Amateur Magician's Handbook.* Its influence is possibly far greater than the previous two, for they are mainly known within the confines of the magic world. *The Amateur Magician's Handbook* was published for the general public. As the author himself has written, his book—as with his previous three books on magic—arose out of a popular publisher's series and not out of the author's overflowing genius. But it is an inspired book nevertheless, full of depth and detail, and for nearly fifty years it taught the basics to generations of would-be magicians.

The author was Henry Hay, the pen name of June Barrows Mussey, who was born in Staten Island, New York, on March 30, 1910. Mussey's father was a professor of economics and his mother, Mabel Hay Barrows, was, in the words of her son, "a dominant personality with all kinds of dramatic, artistic and international brotherhood interests." These same character traits also applied to her son.

Mussey's Christian name, June, was taken from his maternal grandfather, Samuel June Barrows. For the first thirty years of Mussey's life he seemed to struggle with this given identity, calling himself at various times June Barrows Mussey, Barrows Mussey and J. B. Mussey.

"I came to magic at Christmas, 1920," he wrote, "through a copy of Professor Hoffmann's *Modern Magic.*" Magic was one of two early enthusiasms. The second was actually his first love—the art of the book. Everything having to do with books: designing, typesetting, printing, binding, publishing, reading, writing, translating. Mussey would be involved in all these bookish pursuits most of his life but they would not quite bring him the recognition which came to him in magic. He wrote in a letter to me in 1984, "[This] goes to confirm my thesis that one's greatest successes are likely to be achieved in one's second dearest ambition."

By 1922 his parents were living in Wellesley, Massachusetts, where Mussey established a studio for printing and also became a professional magician—both at his mother's urging. He was twelve years old.

"I spent some months of Saturdays in the job

[printing] department of the Ellis Company on Congress Street in Boston," he recalled, "learning to set type and run a press." His parents soon bought him a press of his own. His mother wanted him to call it "The Merrymount Press" in emulation of the famous Boston printing firm of the same name, owned and operated by Daniel Berkeley Updike. She sent the reluctant boy to ask Updike's blessing on this new enterprise and, not surprisingly, Updike said no. So Mussey's press became The Merrythought Press. On it he printed stationery, greeting cards and booklets of poetry. He also produced handbills and tickets to promote his career as Hajji Baba the Magician.

The name and the outfit—bloused shirt, sash and Turkish turban—had most likely been inspired by the famous 19th-century book *Adventures of Hajji Baba of Ispahan.* The tricks he performed were somewhat less exotic. He cut up and restored his turban, and from a silk hat produced a can of tomatoes, handkerchiefs and a ringing alarm clock. He was especially adept at sleight of hand feats with coins. He began performing for church and charity affairs, and during the summers spent several weeks touring on his own. In a letter to a magician friend, he stated, "One summer when I went on tour to New England summer camps at $25 a show, I made 90 bucks some weeks, which my mother re-

COMING!

HAJJI BABA THE MAGICIAN

EXHIBITION EXTRAORDINARY of mysteries and marvels manifestly miraculous!

Don't miss this Popular Prestidigitator performing Exploits Exclusive and Unexcelled!

See him, and he cheats your eyes;
Miss him, and you cheat yourself!

Merrythought Press

Self-printed handbill for the twelve-year-old boy wonder June Barrows Mussey, about 1922.

marked was better than my father's pay as a professor of economics at Wellesley."

In 1924, before his fourteenth birthday, he left high school and embarked on a solo grand tour. According to *The Amateur Magician's Handbook,* the tour was set up by friends of his family who "arranged for full-scale performances in eight or nine cities between Boston and Iowa." The cities included New York, Chicago and Milwaukee. In Iowa he went to Marshalltown to meet his boyhood idol, T. Nelson Downs, who, as a master of coin manipulation, had played vaudeville in England and the States billed as "The King of Koins." Downs and John Mulholland, a society magician and editor of *The Sphinx,* were the chief influences in Mussey's magic career, and references to them appear in all of his books.

Here is how he described the next two years of his life: "In December of 1924 I set out alone for a tour of Europe that ran until April. The official purposes were printing and my other absorbing hobby, conjuring. It involved visits to family friends in Germany, Czechoslovakia, France and England, and a month's stay in Nurnberg, Germany, where I worked as a trainee or tolerated onlooker in a printing plant. The following winter I went to Europe again, this time with my mother. That fall I entered Haverford College."

He was sixteen by then and studied at Haverford two years. In 1929 his parents moved to New York City and Mussey transferred to Columbia University. He met John Mulholland and, according to Mussey's recollection in *The Amateur Magician's Handbook,* he was given the run of the Mulholland apartment. Mussey graduated from Columbia in 1930, Phi Beta Kappa, at the age of twenty and promptly went off to visit Europe again.

Mulholland became the editor of *The Sphinx* in May 1930, when he was thirty-two years old. An article appeared in the May issue titled "Magical English" which instructed magicians on how to speak properly while performing. The author was June Barrows Mussey. The following month a more philosophical piece appeared—"Why Do You Do Magic?"—by J. B. Mussey. In the July and August issues Mussey reported on the magic scene in Germany, based on his most recent European trip. Decades later Mussey described this period as time he spent as *The Sphinx*'s managing editor, although there is no mention of a such a position on the magazine's masthead. No doubt his familiarity with pre-press layout and printing was a help to Mulholland as *The Sphinx* was redesigned in a more modern format. In turn Mulholland, perhaps by conveying the informal title of managing editor on Mussey, encouraged the young graduate in his efforts to find a place in the publishing world. It may have also been through Mulholland that Mussey could later claim to have met and known dozens of important figures on the magic scene.

Varying accounts are given as to how Mussey met Fulton Oursler, the longtime editor-in-chief of *Liberty* magazine and an avid amateur magician. Either on a ship bound for Europe or at a meeting of the Magician's Club in London, the two met and became friends. They soon collaborated on the English-language edition of Ottokar Fischer's *Das Wunderbuch der Zauberkunst,* originally published in Stuttgart in 1929. The first American edition was published in 1931 by the well-known trade publisher Macmillan under the title *Illustrated Magic.* Mussey is credited as translator and Oursler as editor. The book ran through many printings in the 1930s and remained in print for nearly three decades. Although it is not likely Mussey earned much in royalties from this translation, it can be considered the first of his string of successful magic books.

During the years 1930 to 1938, Mussey found and lost several jobs in publishing and became a publisher himself. His longest job seems to have been as secretary to Albert Boni, of the New York firm Albert and

Charles Boni. "Probably very few publishing hopefuls have enjoyed such an all-around short course in the trade," he recalled years later. He continued writing occasional articles for *The Sphinx,* including "Doing Magic for the Public" (by J. B. Mussey) and "Thomas Nelson Downs: A Note" (by Barrows Mussey). In a capsule biography in the September 1932 issue, he is listed as a "pro" specializing in coin magic.

"Early in 1933," he recalled, "Boni's sales manager, Percy Loring, and I started a publishing house on a paid-in capital of $40. . . . As I look back, the high points of my publishing career were the days when the first carton of a new title arrived from the bindery." One of these high points, not only for Mussey but for students of magic history, was the appearance of *John Mulholland's Story of Magic,* which the firm of Loring & Mussey published in 1935. The designer of this handsome volume was Barrows Mussey, who had this to say about the book: "*Mulholland's Story of Magic* was created to exploit the illustrations John had used in *The Sphinx.* There is a severe booboo in it that John caught too late: Mohammed Baksh the 'Hindu' was of course a Mohammedan from what became Pakistan."

The firm Loring & Mussey became Barrows Mussey, Inc., after Loring went to work for another publisher. Mussey's first marriage had taken place by then and his wife helped him in the business. Unfortunately, by late 1936, near the height of the Depression, the business was failing and Mussey took a job with Robert M. McBride, whom he described as "an established but notoriously incompetent publisher." He took another job in the spring of 1937 while his wife, in his words, "wound up the Mussey business." These were not easy times. He later wrote: "[My wife and I] were separated just when I was getting fired in early 1938 and this ended my career as a typographically concerned publisher. I turned to translating books for a living. . . ."

He had, of course, been busy at this pursuit for some time. In a 1984 article in *Publishers Weekly* Mussey summed up his career as a translator: "For a dozen years I earned a living, barely, from 50-hour weeks of translating, plus [reading manuscripts for publishers]. I couldn't have done either in just one language. [In all I spent] fifty years translating—nearly 70 books from eight languages. . . ."

He also took up another career, as a ghostwriter. He wrote to fellow magician Richard Hatch in 1982: "Scribners has reissued John Mulholland's *Beware Familiar Spirits,* much of which . . . I wrote." Evidence of this can be found in the book, which was first published by Charles Scribner's Sons in 1938. Here is a sample, and a good example of Mussey's wit and writing style:

"Although the theatrical effect of the performance is good, [spiritualistic] materialization has peculiar drawbacks for fraudulent mediums. Detection is easier, and the victim's indignation greater. The Reverend J. S. Barrows, grandfather of my friend Barrows Mussey, attended such a seance in Boston, accompanied by a believer, a General who had lost his wife, and by a student from the Massachusetts Institute of Technology. At the seance, the General's wife (who had been tall and slender, with a pronounced Southern accent) returned to earth in a short, dumpy figure, with a breath smelling of garlic. The M.I.T. man then asked to see his sister Caroline. He talked with her at some length, finally saying that he was doubly glad to know her since this was the first he had learned of her existence. Doctor Barrows then seized Caroline's wrist, and began counting her pulse. He did so, despite her struggles, until the medium, discreetly showing a blackjack, said, 'Let go her hand, or I'll hurt you.' This was an actionable threat, so Doctor Barrows said, 'Normal [pulse]; thank you,' and left the seance."

The first and only magic book to appear under Mussey's own name was titled simply *Magic* and was one of a series of books in "Barnes Idle Hour Library," which included other titles on chess, fist puppetry, dancing, checkers, etc. It is a compilation of eighty tricks ranging from close-up feats to parlor effects. The book might be best described as a mixture of magic, stunts, puzzles and con games. The too-few illustrations in the book show the author's hands in action.

"With longer experience in the practical side of magic," a reviewer noted, "Barrows Mussey should be able to write a work of more enduring value than the present volume." The critic was both right and wrong in this regard. Better books were to come from Mussey, but the present volume did very well. Within the first year of its publication it went through at least six printings.

By the time *Magic* was published in 1942, Mussey was in the Marine Corps, commissioned as a captain, and working in an air intelligence unit. When he was released from service in 1945 he resumed work as a foreign-language reader for publishing houses. The next five years, however, included much more than reading the manuscripts of other authors. It was one of the most productive periods of his career. In those few years he wrote three popular magic books and compiled several anthologies of New England folkways which were illustrated from his vast collection of antique woodcuts.

The first of the books was *Learn Magic,* issued in 1947 and one of a series advertised as "Superb Book Values at Low Prices." The author was listed as Henry Hay. According to Mussey's widow, Dagmar, the contract with A. S. Barnes had stipulated that Mussey's next book be offered to them first. Barnes, however, turned down *Learn Magic,* either because it did not fit the firm's current publishing program or perhaps because the editors felt it covered too much of the same material presented in *Magic.* The publishers also were not in favor of having another magic book appear under Mussey's name with a different firm. Mussey solved the problem by taking the pen name Henry Hay, after his maternal great-grandfather.

"Learn Magic For Fun and Popularity," the cover of the book declared. "The magician's basic tricks explained step-by-step in twenty simple lessons." Despite the lesson format, *Learn Magic* is anything but formal. The order of the lessons is arbitrary and Mussey's approach is casual, conversational and full of asides—as if he were leaning over your shoulder giving you one-on-one training. He also left little for the student to guess at. If there was a right way and a wrong way to do something, he pointed out both.

Editions of *Learn Magic* were published in Canada and the United Kingdom. In 1949 a Perma Giants

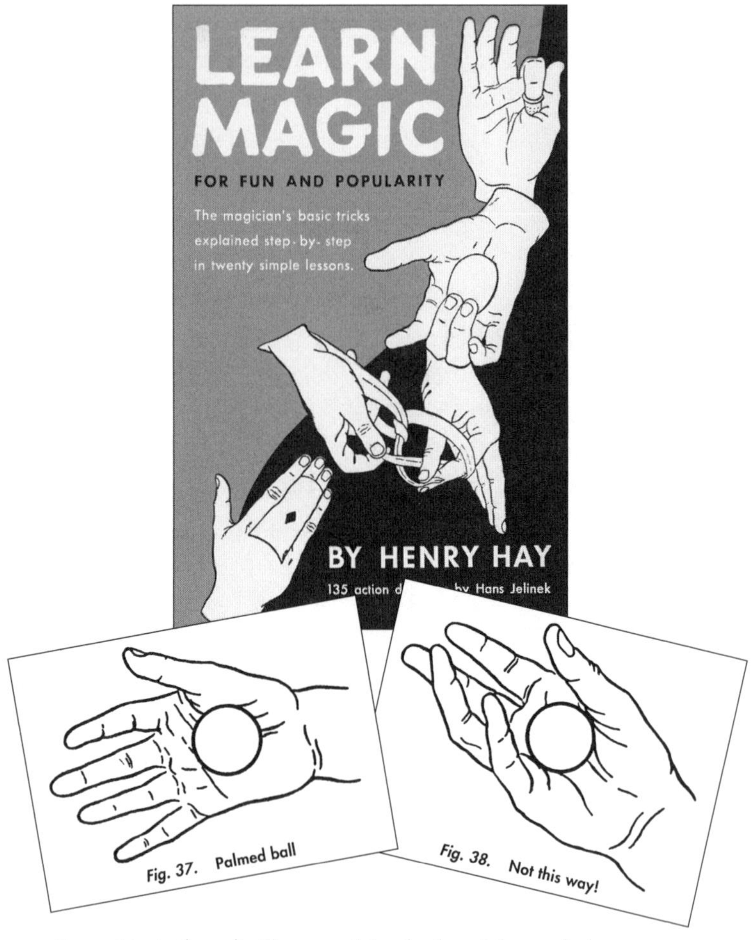

Learn Magic (1947) illustrated both the right and the wrong way to perform certain sleight-of-hand movements.

edition (an oversized offspring of a paperback) was issued and likely to have been sold through drugstore and newsstand outlets. Mussey translated the book in the mid-1970s for a German publisher. *Learn Magic* was reprinted in 1975 with a new introduction and minor revisions by the author and the book has been in print ever since.

Mussey's *Cyclopedia of Magic,* "edited by Henry Hay," was published in 1949. It is based on the writings and performances of the twenty-eight magicians who are listed on the title page and of many others who are mentioned in the text. Twenty-nine "classic" magic books are cited as sources, some of which their authors never intended for circulation outside of the magic world. All information appears in alphabetical order. If Mussey had known about the yet-to-be-invented Zig-Zag Girl illusion in 1949, his *Cyclopedia* might have been complete from A to Z. Actually it covers only A to Y, the last entry being a trick titled "You Do As I Do." The beginning entry concerns the archaic term "acquitment: any sleight for showing both hands empty when actually something is concealed. Most acquitments are as labored as their name." An amusing entry is listed as "Sleeve, Up His." Brief biographies of 50 magicians are included.

Mussey harbored no particular feeling for or pride

in the book. In a 1985 letter, he had this to say about it: "*Cyclopedia of Magic* was dreamed up for the benefit of the publisher, whose printer then declined to do the make-up and left it all to me. . . . I haven't seen the book in forty-odd years."

At the same time he was assembling the *Cyclopedia,* he must have been writing *The Amateur Magician's Handbook.* Photographs of Mussey's hands demonstrating sleights and moves appear in both books. Forty-four photographs appeared in the *Cyclopedia* and 198 in the *Handbook.* There is no duplication of photos between the books.

The Amateur Magician's Handbook was published in 1950, one year after the *Cyclopedia.* Like his previous books, it appeared in a series, this one under the heading of "Basic Handbooks." Other titles in the series were devoted to amateur photography, stamp collecting and ham radio operation. *The Handbook* incorporated material which had appeared in the *Cyclopedia.* In fact, each of Mussey's magic books was a reworking of earlier books, both his own and others, but each was completely rewritten from Mussey's own experience and point of view—not a mere plagiarizing of his own or other writers' works.

As a teaching tool, the *Handbook* is Mussey's best effort. Its value lies not only in the tricks Mussey chose

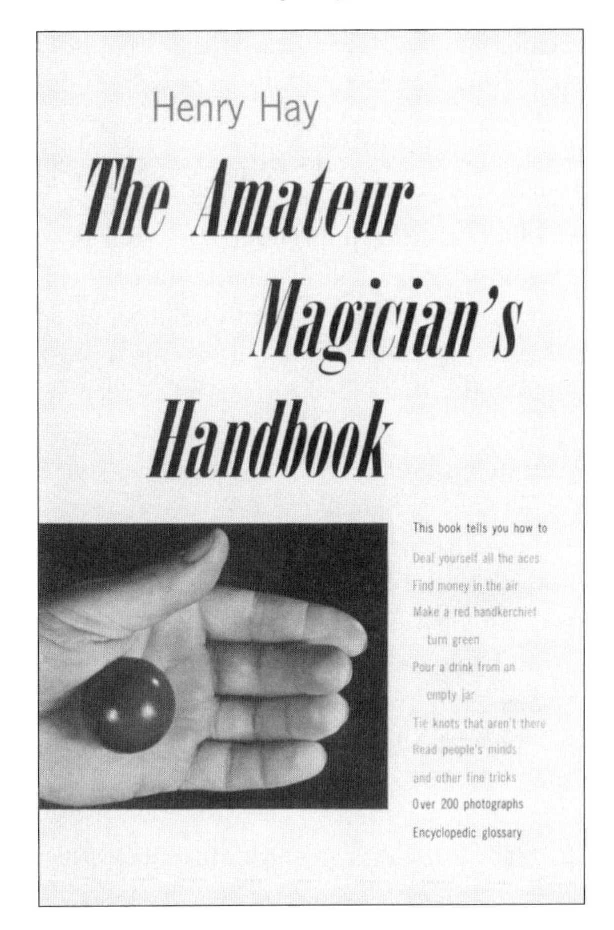

Dust jacket cover for the first edition of *The Amateur Magician's Handbook* (1950), a book which remained in print in updated versions for the next fifty years.

to include, but also in the extraordinary steps he takes to teach them. In addition to giving methods, he often discusses attitude, philosophy, psychology and any other scrap he can come up with to help the beginner perform successfully. The insider information to help the budding magician understand why a trick is worth performing, what resistance he might encounter from his audience, even what failures might occur, probably makes the *Handbook* unique among books for beginners. Still, it was less than a best seller in the beginning.

A second, expanded edition did not appear until 1965, fifteen years after the first. By that time Mussey had been living and working in Germany for fifteen years. He had initially moved there to become the German correspondent for the New York *Journal of Commerce.* Then, as he described it, "I've drifted into advertising." He also met and married his German wife, Dagmar, an advertising consultant. He found his new life satisfying.

Throughout the printing history of *The Amateur Magician's Handbook,* Mussey was updating and correcting shortcomings or mistakes of earlier editions. He said he had to refresh old conjuring friendships and call on new pen pals for help in revising the original work. In the *Handbook,* as in his previous books, T. Nelson

Downs and John Mulholland figure prominently as sages and innovators. The dedication page of the first and second editions reads, "In memoriam THOMAS NELSON DOWNS 'The Great Man' of my boyhood." Added to this in the third edition was "And, alas, JOHN MULHOLLAND. What shall we do without him?" The third edition, revised and expanded again, appeared in 1972, both in hardcover and paperback. Over 100,000 copies of the paperback edition were eventually sold.

By the time the newly revised and expanded fourth edition appeared in 1982, the original publisher of *The Amateur Magician's Handbook* had been merged into a larger corporation. The new edition featured added sections on shows for children and a then-new phenomenon, videotape. It also contains a revision to the Ten-Card Trick with the acknowledgment: "Profuse thanks to my friend Richard Hatch, the first reader in over 30 years to spot a blunder at this point in the original description of the trick." This was the final updated edition of *The Amateur Magician's Handbook.* The book has remained in print, however, as a discounted "remainder."

Although Mussey's name was still to be seen in bookstores, time and distance eventually obscured his memory. An article in a magic magazine in the early

1970s asked readers to help identify the boy who had traveled around the country in the 1920s wearing a turban and calling himself Hajji Baba. Several magicians responded and the result was a follow-up article by Mussey on his boyhood visit with T. Nelson Downs. Richard Hatch and I, and others enamored of Mussey's writing, sought him out in our own ways. Hatch visited the Musseys at their home in Dusseldorf, Germany; a half-finished letter to him was in the typewriter the day Mussey died at age seventy-five on July 27, 1985.

Mussey and I had planned to meet that September. We had been corresponding for several years and he intended to write a new introduction to my reprint of a book he had ghostwritten in 1950. This was Charles P. Everitt's *The Adventures of a Treasure Hunter: A Rare Bookman in Search of American History.* Mussey explained to me how the book was written. "My contract with [the publisher] included all the bourbon [the author] could drink, and in the course of writing I actually bought two or three cases of Old Granddad. It was a relatively moral arrangement because I, being a rum-drinker, did not take more than a glass an evening of the private stock, for sociability." I would have liked to have had Barrows Mussey's full story of the writing of this book, but I had to republish without it.

Barrows Mussey. (Courtesy of Dagmar Mussey.)

"It used to be a parlor game to ask people what historical figure they would like to have been," he wrote to me in a letter in March 1984. "I would rather wonder what figure they might probably have been. Myself I have an obscure hero, Samuel Griswold Goodrich (pen name: Peter Parley), who failed twice as a publisher before becoming the most successful American writer of juveniles of his day, and spent some of his last years in France, international-publishing away. But we might turn the game forward to find that you are the person I might most likely have become . . . publisher and rare-book dealer."

As we can see, Barrows Mussey was so much more.

Generation Lux

IN OCTOBER 1928, Vernon Edward Lux, twenty-two years old and living in Niles, Ohio, submitted his handwriting to be "analyzed" by *Detective Fiction Weekly,* a pulp magazine located at 280 Broadway, New York City.

"Your handwriting shows you are conscientious in whatever you undertake," began the personally typed letter he received in reply. "The straightforwardness of character which is so evident in you is the key to the door of your success. . . . Better give your ambitions full speed ahead."

This he obviously did. News clippings of the period tell of Lux working in the composing room of the *Niles Daily Times* and, having "started in the magic-making business when just a boy living in Oregon [Illinois]," he was also presenting magic shows. In 1929 a *Daily Times* story about a party given for forty newsboys stated that they had eaten over two hundred sandwiches, eight cakes, four gallons of ice cream, dozens of hot chocolates and had been entertained by Vernon Lux, "The Master of Magic."

By 1932 he was back in Illinois. His father, Fred E. Lux, and other family members were running a newspaper in Rochelle, a small town a hundred miles west of Chicago. When Lux was not working as a printer for the paper, he was performing as "Mysterious Ed" in schools and theatres in nearby towns.

"With the aid of a number of small boys from the audience he baked a cake in a hat, made a haunted clock stop at any number called for . . . , made bottles, eggs, balls, fish bowls, flags and many other articles disappear and appear at will." Forty years later the apparatus for these miracles, well worn and stuffed in boxes or wrapped in newspapers, was found in the basement of his home in Mount Morris, Illinois.

One of the great outdoor attractions of the 1930s was the blindfold automobile drive.

"HOW CAN IT BE DONE?" read the full-page ad in *The Franklin* [Illinois] *Reporter.* "See LUX drive a Ford car, while blindfolded, through the streets of Franklin Grove, Saturday afternoon. Join the crowd at Fruit's Garage at 2:00 o'clock. Assist in blindfolding this man of mystery and see him drive away in a car furnished by this active Ford dealer. During the drive, the Magician will make stops at the following places, who kindly co-operated by advertising on this page. . . ." Fox Musical Instruments, Blackhawk Produce Company, D & W Ice Cream, Herbst Feed Company and the American Legion Post were among the sponsors.

Lux performed this stunt with considerable success and cleverness. Not only did he "obey all traffic rules" while driving blindfolded, he ended on a definite high note—by driving the car onto a hydraulic lift which raised it above the crowd. And how did he ensure that a crowd would be gathered? "An artist from the Gullickson Studio will be present . . . to take photographs of the crowds . . . which will be published later. You are invited to be among those present. Remember the hour, 2 P.M. sharp."

In 1942 Lux prepared a written explanation for his method of performing what he called The Lux "Supreme" Blindfold Drive: "The blindfold is unprepared, except that it has a strip of elastic tape, instead of cords . . . allowing the blindfold to be lowered. The bag is prepared so you can see through it." Careful instructions explain how to "scrape the fuzz off the velveteen" of the two bags used to cover the head. The bags have been sewn together "with the fuzz side sewed inside." In performance, this bag is first slipped over the head of the person examining the blindfolds. The see-through side of the bag is at the rear of the examiner's head. "Now remove bag from his head, and hold it in your hands without turning it around—so

(Above) A hooded Vernon Lux pauses before beginning a "blindfold drive" in front of his sponsor's auto dealership. *(Below)* For the spectacular finish, the car was hoisted in the air. The conjuror, still in the driver's seat, and his spectators then posed for a photograph which would be published in the local newspaper.

when bag is slipped on YOUR head, the prepared side is to the FRONT. As your hands pass down the sides of your head under cover of the bag, your thumbs grasp the sides of the blindfold and pull it down away from your eyes."

A few precautions were included:

"It is good SHOWMANSHIP to have someone LEAD you to the car and HELP you in!"

"It is a good plan, when performing this drive to secure the permission of the authorities in the town where the drive is to be presented."

"DRIVE CAREFULLY!—as the LAW will hold you responsible in case of any accident, even though it may be doubtful that it was your fault!"

Lux advised that he had "used this system for 16 years [since 1926] without the slightest mishap!"

His magic act, consisting of a dozen standard tricks, included the Vanishing Wand and Walking Through a Ribbon. After his marriage he was assisted by his wife, Effie, and later his young daughter, Doris Dee, joined the show, which he called "In Wonderland." His featured illusion, which he called the "Chinese Death Cabinet," consisted of a large upright box in which his wife stood as "thirty-six swords and steel plates are thrust through all directions and may be seen protruding from sides and back." On occasion he also escaped from the "Siberian Transport Cage. The only one in this country! Imported from Europe."

Working in the printing trade, Lux made good use of its resources. Brochures, handbills, window cards, posters and blotters promoted his show. Tickets for individual performances were often issued. A "School Child's Ticket" was printed on a square of card stock twice the size of a child's hand. Lux had at least half a dozen different business cards and several varieties of stationery.

Will Goldston's 1934 London publication, *Who's Who In Magic,* listed Lux in the section devoted to professional magicians. Lux's favorite magician was Cardini; his favorite trick, the Multiplying Billiard Balls; his favorite author, (naturally) Will Goldston. He was also reported to be "the Organizer and President [of the] International Society of Junior Magicians."

Lux's International Society of Junior Magicians was organized in 1932, and grew to "a fraternity of several thousand members," according to the letter of introduction from the Office of the President. By the time it was all over, fourteen years later, nearly five thousand youngsters and adults had come and gone as members of the ISJM.

The purpose of Lux's magic club was to bring together, through the pages of its "Official Organ, *The*

School Child's
TICKET
This Ticket and 10c will Admit
One School Child to
"WONDERLAND"
Presented By
V. E. LUX & CO.
"The Master of Magic"
at the Rose Theatre,
BYRON
Saturday, Nov. 22d, 8 p.m.

Vernon Lux's connection with a family newspaper business allowed him to print posters, handbills, letterheads, ink blotters, calling cards and other publicity pieces to advertise his magic show. This whimsical "ticket"—printed on heavy card stock and measuring 4¾″ by 5¾″—was sure to be larger than the child's hand holding it.

Dragon," magicians who were "denied admittance," because of their youth, into other magic clubs. The membership fee was twenty-five cents; yearly dues were one dollar, for which one received a membership card and twelve issues of the club's publication. Classified ads in *Popular Science, Popular Mechanics* and other magazines quickly swelled the ranks of the ISJM.

"I had a job that kept me busy only 40 hours a week," Lux wrote in an undated article sometime in the 1940s. "I enjoyed spending another four hours a day writing letters to friends, writing copy [for *The Dragon*], and publishing the magazine. I am a printer and did a great deal of the work myself. The small subscription fee . . . barely paid postage, paper, and the small amount of additional help I needed. . . ."

Lux's other enterprises, established and operated in conjunction with the magic club, may have been more profitable. One of these was a mail-order magic business. First called The L & L Magic Company and later The Lux Magic Studio, it offered pocket and parlor effects, from top-of-the-line apparatus built by craftsmen to fifty-cent mysteries commonly called "slum magic." Lux's ads for tricks and magic books appeared in *The Dragon* and were collected and reissued as catalogs. ISJM members received a ten-percent discount off the list prices. The Specialty Shop—"Printing of All Kinds—Magicians' Supplies"—operated through a post office box in Oregon, Illinois, and featured used magic books and apparatus in the club's magazine. Vernon Lux did not advertise the fact that this was another of his businesses.

Members of the ISJM became familiar with another Lux club:

"Are you enjoying the benefits of the Magic Rental Library? It enables you to read many magic books at low cost. Membership fee in the Library Club is $1.00, and a book deposit of $2.00 is required. This book deposit will be returned at any time requested. The books are sent postpaid and you are allowed to keep them 2 weeks for the low minimum rental fee."

The rental library was a bargain for young magicians who could not afford to buy every magic book they wanted. Rentals ran from twenty to fifty cents, plus three cents each additional day over two weeks. (There were exceptions to this rule. One of Will Goldston's famous "locked books," the mammoth, four-hundred-page, limited, numbered edition of *Great Magicians' Tricks,* required a ten-dollar deposit fee before being sent.)

While the rental concept was popular with ISJM members, the idea was not appreciated in all quarters. In September 1940 Percy Abbott, owner of Abbott's Magic Company, wrote in response to a order for books from Lux: "It is our understanding that you rent these books out, and this is against our principles. We are therefore returning your check. . . ."

The rental library consisted of over eight hundred books, pamphlets, printed manuscripts, illusion plans—even magazines. Each was affixed with a manila clasp envelope pasted inside, which held a library card. Lux was not averse to renting books which had either been given or autographed to him. A copy of *Houdini's Paper Magic*—"To Mr. Vernon Lux (an old newspaper man who's hobby now is good magic), I inscribe my name with best personal wishes, Mrs. Harry Houdini"—became a part of the rental library. The worn condition of the rental books attests to their frequent travels through the mails and their use by youthful readers.

The members, young and old, came from all parts of the world—wherever those magazines in which he advertised happened to be read.

"Like so many others of our generation," Sid Fleischman wrote, "I discovered the tuxedoed Pied Piper of magic-smitten boys of those sunlit days—Vernon E. Lux. I joined the International Society of Junior Magicians and began to submit original notions to its publication, *The Dragon.*" Fleischman, author of the best-selling children's book *Mr. Mysterious & Company* and numerous others, joined the ISJM at the age of thirteen. In his application for membership, dated November 17, 1933, he stated that he had been interested in magic since he was eleven when he "personally" met a magician at a sideshow. He was nominated for membership in the club by his friend Buddy Ryan, who received a dime credit on his own dues for recruiting young Fleischman. "The boy is very nice and mighty clever with thimbles," Ryan wrote. Fleischman was given Membership Number 481.

The questions Lux asked on the application for membership were specific. In addition to name, address and occupation, there were other blanks to fill in: "My first association with Magic began about ________ and at ________. Professional Name (if any) ________. I am a Collector of ________. I am a member of the following Magic Societies ________. I heard of the ISJM through ________. . . ."

Over four thousand applications offer biographical details not only about a generation of American magicians who grew up in the 1930s and '40s, but about many who had become established performers by that time. John Booth (nightclub magician), George Marquis (stage illusionist), Ed Reno (old-time Chautauqua performer), John "Have-A-Laf" Walker (sideshow magician), Will Nicola (world-traveling illusionist), Joe Ovette (Canadian magician) and Sorcar (India's great illusionist) were among the professional showmen who joined the ISJM. George A. Holly, sixty-two years old and retired when he joined, had been a magician in 1889 with a unit of the Kickapoo Medicine Show in Indiana. Honorary Members included Mrs. Houdini and T. Nelson Downs, "the king" of coin magic. But not every member was a magician. Edwin Francis Wilson was a famous actor whose first association with magic occurred in "1911 when I was with Miss Maude Adams in *Peter Pan*."

Equally impressive are the young magicians whose names have since become familiar on the magic scene. George Johnstone, Al Delage and Neil Foster would eventually become professional magicians. Gerald Andrus, who became a noted innovator of close-up magic, listed his occupation as "school boy" when he joined the ISJM at age sixteen, four years after witnessing the performance of a reformed spiritualist medium. Robert Harkness Parrish, Jr., had become interested in magic in "1928 or thereabouts . . . at the age of 10 after reading my first magic book." He went on to write fourteen magic books, several in collaboration with other members of the ISJM. Sisters Roberta and Marion Byron were already well known as a performing duo at magic conventions when they became members in 1932. David Wagoner joined in 1941; years later he became a well-known poet and wrote the novel *The Escape Artist*.

Filling in the blank for "Professional Name" inspired many young members to flights of fancy. George Johnstone, at age fifteen, wanted to be called "Professor George Houdin." Kenneth Earl Wilhite was "Professor Fool'em Easy." Donne Brian Anthony James Richard Murphy called himself "Murdon the Magician." Thomas Warner wrote "El Macroni"—then added "No longer used." Thomas David Pinchong wrote, "I am Chinese. Please give me a name."

Applications to membership in a club are not meant to give clues to the outcome of personal lives. However, by reading those sent to Lux decades after the fact, a sharp eye can sometimes detect a personal tragedy which was to follow. Ronald Perry joined the ISJM in 1942, at age twelve. He called himself "Mr. Fi." Forty years later, a much-published and respected poet, he committed suicide. Albert Joseph Jefferson posted his application to Lux from Pearl Harbor on June 23, 1941. He was a twenty-four-year-old enlisted man on Admiral Kimmel's command ship, *U.S.S. Honolulu.* The cruiser was strafed, bombed and flooded on December 7th, the morning the Japanese attacked. What became of Jefferson is not known.

The success of the ISJM was due as much to the efforts of its youthful members as to those of Vernon Lux. While he provided *The Dragon,* a newsprint-quality publication, on a monthly basis, the members filled many of its sixteen- to twenty-four-page issues with news, opinions, tricks and ideas.

In the October 1938 issue, nineteen-year-old book reviewer/columnist Robert Parrish wrote, "I [have] volunteered, at the request of nobody, to offer a list of recommended books from the stand point of the beginner." Having read magic books for nearly ten years, Parrish wisely cautioned readers with this insight: "If one believes all the claims which are made for each new addition to the extensive literature of magic, he is going to be in for a lot of disillusionment . . . he should remember that magical ad writers, above all other magi, are adept at misdirection."

Oscar Weigle, Jr., was another active contributor. A third of the April 1938 issue of *The Dragon* was written by Weigle. "Clever Conjuring" (later titled "Themes and Schemes") was his own column and "Magic For Beginners" was written with another teenage member. Weigle later became a highly regarded editor in book publishing. George Johnstone—by then calling himself "Dr. Houdaille"—was among many who took turns as ISJM contributors. "Young enthusiasts from around the country," magic historian Jim Alfredson has written, "[shared] their experience—and inexperience" in the pages of *The Dragon.*

In 1942 Vernon Lux identified himself on his

newest business card as "Printer-Magician" and "Delegate" to a typographical union convention held in Colorado. This was one of several excursions into politics. He developed a "Lux Campaign Plan" during this period for the benefit of the Republican party. "A series of rallies has been designed with the idea of reaching the ordinary citizen—the merchants, townsmen and farmers who do not ordinarily attend rallies, but who must be won over to the party if we are to win this fall. . . . The Lux & Co. show will create a lot of good will. . . ." Letters from state candidates thanked Lux for his efforts, though none mention magic shows having been a part of their election campaigns.

"In 1945 I went into the electrical appliance business and quit printing," Lux wrote. "I had planned on just doing the editorial work on *The Dragon* and hiring the complete print job done, but . . . each month the print bill got bigger. . . . I had to work ten hours a day, six days a week! So *The Dragon* died."

With it went the International Society of Junior Magicians, The Rental Library Club, The Lux Magic Studio and The Specialty Shop of Oregon, Illinois. They were replaced by the Dee-Lux Repair Shop, set up in Lux's garage.

For a while he conducted a column called "Dragon Reincarnate," for the magic magazine *The New Tops,* in which he reminisced about earlier times and published tricks and ideas which had been submitted to *The Dragon* but were never used. Letters and membership dues addressed to the ISJM were still arriving in Mount Morris and orders were coming in for the Magic Studio—but they were not opened. Envelopes with coins, dollars and money orders still enclosed were set aside and never answered. Vernon E. Lux, though he may never have lost his enthusiasm for magic, had grown tired of the enterprises he had been engaged in for the past seventeen years.

The brief obituaries following his death in 1962 at the age of fifty-six failed to mention his clubs and businesses which had nurtured a generation of magicians who were, by the time of his death, at the forefront of magic.

In the early 1980s the remnants of Lux's magic company, records of The International Society of Junior Magicians, files of *The Dragon* and eight hundred well-worn volumes comprising The Magic Rental Library Club were put up for sale. These enterprises had been housed in the basement and garage of their founder, owner and operator. Like many other cottage-industry magic businesses, they had flourished, languished and disappeared without notice. Unlike others who operated such businesses, Lux had brought together a generation of young, would-be magicians, encouraged their interest, fostered friendships among them, and enabled them to express and share their ideas and aspirations in print. The significance of Lux's contribution to magic was never fully recognized in his lifetime. Perhaps he never realized it himself.

Fran and Me

THE LADY BEHIND THE COUNTER of the magic shop addressed me as "my boy." She was about forty and I was about twelve. Her name was Frances Marshall; she was the widow of the shop's founder, Laurie Ireland, and wife of the well-known magician Jay Marshall. The time was the mid-1950s when my grandmother Grace and I would ride the South Shore commuter train from Northwest Indiana for a day of shopping in Chicago. It was a wonderfully active era for magic in the city during those years. Not staying out late at that age, I won't pretend to have seen the many magicians who played the nightclubs or entertained in the hotel bars. My memories are of trailing my grandmother as she roamed the clothing racks of Marshall Field's and other department stores and, in turn, as she followed me where I wanted to go.

Ireland Magic Company, on the fourth floor of 109 North Dearborn Street, was my favorite stop. Although none of the clothing store employees ever paid any attention to me, Frances Marshall always felt sorry for my grandmother and usually offered her a chair.

There wasn't much standing space, much less sitting room in Frances's small shop, so my grandmother often sat in the hallway, across from the elevators. While I gazed at the splendid array of magic displayed in the showcases and lined along shelves on the walls behind, other customers coming and going must have wondered whose grandmother was guarding the door.

"My boy," Frances addressed me, as she no doubt called many others who peered across the counter. How could she help me? Well, I had seen Don Alan perform a certain effect on his *Magic Ranch* show on television, or I had read an ad in *Genii* magazine about a new trick or I had learned about a classic in my favorite book, *Cyclopedia of Magic* by Henry Hay. Frances dug out a version of what I was after and the sale was closed.

She was not one to stand about waiting for further business or to lean across the counter to peddle an unwanted trick. Neither was a twelve-year-old ready to leave a magic shop after purchasing what he had come for. If she was satisfied that you were content to keep on looking, she disappeared through the small doorway that led to rooms in the back. Intriguing and inviting was that doorway, leading, in my mind, to an ever more wondrous cache of magic. You had to believe that, because you were never invited back there

Frances Marshall in her shop at 109 N. Dearborn Street, Chicago, about 1950. She is demonstrating one of the most popular magic effects of the time, The Chinese Bottle Trick.

and it never seemed that Frances would come out again unless you called her, which I was too shy to do. She always did come back eventually. Another customer arrived or she stepped out to check on whether I was still there. I don't know what I thought she must be doing in the back, but I doubt I imagined her doing anything so practical as packing orders to mail to catalog customers.

Her sister Marguerite and for a time Neil Foster, a professional magician, helped Frances in the shop during my youthful visits. They were both kind and friendly to me. Like Frances, Marguerite disappeared into the back room soon after seeing who had come in. Neil delighted in demonstrating magic and seemed genuinely interested in helping a young magician find his way among the numerous effects on the market. He also sold me a much-coveted book, *Magical Rope Ties & Escapes* by Houdini, published half a century earlier in London. I have my copy still.

Regrettably, I can't recall a single magic trick that I bought in all those visits my grandmother and I made, although I can still see that marvelous silver Spirit Trumpet which Frances had displayed in an overhead showcase. I wanted it very much; but she was quick to explain that it wasn't a piece of apparatus a boy magician could effectively use. Had I been able to buy it, the memory of it would not be so vivid to me now. I wonder in whose collection—or attic—it now resides.

What I do remember are the books I bought. This telltale fact is all one needs to know to understand why I became a collector of magic books rather than a magician. My talents as a conjuror matched those of so many others who have come into the fold and then left. The difference is, after learning that I wasn't go-

Book by Houdini, published in London in 1921 and purchased for five dollars at Ireland Magic Shop in the author's youth.

ing to be a great magician, I stayed for the magic of others. And, of course, the books: for whether they be about tricks or about the lives and careers of the tricksters, they contain a magic of their own.

I did not meet Jay Marshall in Frances's shop. He was too busy traveling and performing during those years. I had seen him on Ed Sullivan's television show and had read about him in the magic magazines, for many notices of his "doings" and appearances were written by Frances. She was a columnist for several magazines and turned the spotlight on Jay every chance she could. I was about sixteen when she suggested I visit Jay at their home in Oak Park to see his magic collection. As Jay and I were talking over the phone to arrange a time for me to visit, I asked him what he collected in magic.

"Everything," he replied.

He meant what he said. On entering their house I encountered floor-to-ceiling bookshelves in their living room. These held more magic books than I ever knew existed. It seemed to me that for every book I owned, Jay had one in the American edition and another in the English. Every room was devoted to some segment of his collection, covering not only magic but all fields of show business and other subjects which interested him. Although Frances was not at the house, her presence was evident. A note on the refrigerator told Jay what to offer me for lunch. Another sign, hanging on a doorknob, read: "Jay, Don't bring David into this room." We caught sight of the sign as we were leaving that room.

The next time I visited the Marshalls, I was in college and they had recently moved their home and business to the north side of Chicago. The company name had changed from Ireland's to Magic, Inc. I came with a pickup truck full of books and magic apparatus to sell Jay and stayed to eat a watermelon which Frances carved on their screened-in porch. Jay in his usual candid and direct manner asked me why I was selling my magic. I don't know what my answer was (it is only his question which sticks in my memory), but I believe I felt that it was time to rid myself of the things of my boyhood and get on with the pursuits of an adult, which for me meant love and literature. I did not realize at the time that I was not going to outgrow magic.

I did not see them again until several years later, perhaps to sell Jay more books. During my previous visit I had marveled at how much space they had on the two floors of their "new" building. The magic shop on the first floor included packing, shipping and storage areas, a printing press, woodworking shop and a

Frances and Jay Marshall in the living room of their home in Oak Park, Illinois, in 1959.

little theatre. Their living quarters and a vast room for Jay's growing collections covered the entire second floor. This time I marveled at how fast all the space had filled up—with the growing magic and publishing business and Jay's ever-expanding accumulations. I was in the army by then: love and literature, like magic, had been temporarily set aside. I was about to begin my tour of duty in Viet Nam. Frances gave me the names of several magicians she knew who were already in that part of the world and suggested I get in touch with them. Had I known then that I would also find my way to Australia, Hong Kong and Thailand, they would probably have offered me the names of friends in those countries, too. I was learning that the Marshalls' magic contacts were worldwide.

In the fall of 1973 I spent an afternoon with Jay browsing through his library and talking on many subjects. Since Viet Nam I had lived in various places, tried to write about my war experiences, and, in Jay's words, "lived a spartan life" by scouting for old books and reselling them to dealers. I was clearly on a wandering path and perhaps getting nowhere. Jay seemed to realize this better than I did. He gave me a famous essay to read titled "Acres of Diamonds." Its author, Russell H. Conwell, had traveled the country giving it as a speech (reportedly over 6,100 times!) in the late decades of the 19th century. The story was about a man who roamed the world seeking treasure and finally found it in his own backyard. After reading it, I did not go home and settle down, but my wandering ended because of a better proposition. Jay asked me to come live and work at Magic, Inc.

Many magicians might think otherwise, but for me the Center of the World in magic in the 1970s was

Chicago. Every magic enthusiast, from the famous illusionist to the kid who had just bought his first trick, was in touch with Frances and Jay at Magic, Inc. The shop and, for special events, the little theatre behind it were gathering places for local and visiting magicians, club meetings and an annual magic collectors' convention. Traveling professionals always stopped by; local talent was booked through the shop. The phone rang constantly, for Jay's advice, for Frances to take an order. Mail orders were still being packed by Frances and Marguerite behind the shop, but now with the help of a diffident little man from Wisconsin called Wally, who had somehow made it through fifty years of his life working mostly in magic shops. He was the demonstrator of tricks. Magic props were being built in the workshops "out back" by puppeteer and balloon man John Shirley and Chinese magician De Yip Looey. "Trick Talk," the firm's newsletter, and countless books by magician-authors were being printed, collated and bound by a "family" of neighborhood workers.

In the upstairs warehouse space I slept in a cubbyhole room with walls that did not reach the vast beamed ceiling overhead. It was called "The Charlie Miller Room," when I stayed there, named after a transient sleight of hand master who was taken in by a succession of magicians who loved to watch him perform. Charlie wasn't the only one to have occupied the room before me and many others took their turn there after my departure. I worked in a corner bounded by a maze of towering shelves which held old inventories of props, supplies, boxes full of mimeographed manuscripts and Jay's incomparable, ever-growing collections. Across the room Frances often sat at the typewriter tapping out her monthly columns for the magic magazines or setting type for new books. In another corner a shy and quiet Japanese lady who spoke few words in English was sewing fabric for use in magic effects. As a boy the romance of what's-in-the-backroom of the magic shop had entranced me. Now, at age thirty, I *lived* there.

If it seems as if I recall Frances in too many places at the same time, it is only because she often appeared to be everywhere at once. She worked long days and covered great distances in that building, and one of the functions of the intercom was to try to keep track of her. Someone always needed her, someone was always calling for her advice. Every activity in the business seemed to need her expertise. Reading her earliest books about her life in magic, *You Don't Have To Be Crazy* and *With Frances In Magic Land,* makes it easier to understand: she had worked her way through the Great Depression of the 1930s, she had helped her family, she

"Always working." Frances Marshall in her upstairs office at Magic, Inc., in the 1970s. She was either typing a letter, composing one of her monthly columns for a magic magazine, preparing ad copy for the company's "Trick Talk" newsletter, writing one of her autobiographical works or typesetting a new magic book.

had kept a business alive after the death of Laurie Ireland. She was taking care of more than ever now, including another mouth to feed—mine. (Did I fail to mention that she prepared morning and evening meals for Jay, her brother Johnny, frequent visitors *and* me?)

A curious change in my friendship with Frances took place after I moved in. She forgot my name. I attribute this to the fact that she didn't approve of my being there.

"*You* can come in to eat," she would say to me. "Tell *him* that it's time" is how she spoke about me. I was living there because Jay was having me undertake several projects on Houdini that Frances simply did not think would pan out. (She was right; they never did.) Other magicians had come to dinner before me and stayed for months thereafter. Charlie Miller was merely the most famous. Frances might have had enough of guests who did not have a departure date in their itineraries.

When I wasn't dashing off with Jay to scout through old bookshops or pal along when meeting visiting magicians, I was researching in his library of books, magazines and filing cabinets. Which brings to mind the Marshalls' cat, Twiggy, which was generally unfriendly and feisty, but liked me and often followed me around. It disappeared once for three days. We looked for it everywhere without luck. On the fourth day I happened to return to a filing cabinet where I had been working, and huddled inside the top drawer when I opened it was Twiggy.

One day Frances described me to one of her

friends as a "book snake." It was a delightfully fractured attempt at "book*worm*" and the term stuck to me in friendly circles around Chicago for several years, mostly due to Jay repeating it. This was the first of many instances when I was fortunate to hear Frances utter one of her wonderful malapropisms. Of course, the humor of a malapropism—a word change in a sentence which transforms it into near-nonsense—belongs to the moment it is rendered. Yet several of Frances's best deserve saving, such as the time she told me that Jay had gone to a hotel to watch a boxing match on "short-circuit TV." The word she meant was *closed*-circuit, but she certainly made this bit of news more interesting. In the Midwest we have a franchise convenience store called White Hen. Frances announced: "They're going to open a new White Pigeon down the street." At breakfast one morning she told us that she had just read that U.S. Telephone had been taken over by Sprite. "By Sprint," Jay admonished. "Sprite is a soft drink. Sprint is a telephone company." Another time he was looking at a weather thermometer and Frances asked, "What time is it there?" Or when they planned to catch a certain TV show, she told Jay, "We'll eat it while we're watching supper." These are but samples; Jay and I were always waiting for Frances to do it again.

Midway through my stay Jay flew to England for his usual month of performing and palling around with his many British friends. Frances used such times to increase her workload and to try to regain control of her household. She enlisted my help by asking me how we could get all the piles of Jay's books off the kitchen floor. Nearly all the nearby wall space was already covered with shelved books, so I suggested a new, free-standing bookcase. We purchased one and by the time Jay returned, all his books were off the floor. A year or so later when I entered the kitchen I saw another huge pile of books but no bookcase.

"What happened to the bookcase?" I asked.

"Oh, it's there," Frances said.

Stacks of added books had surrounded and completely covered it.

My Houdini project, which attempted to recount the great showman's day-to-day performances throughout his career, had effectively come to a standstill for lack of information. With Jay in England, I felt more than ever the need to justify my continuing presence. Luckily he had left behind a few unfinished projects of his own, including one which Frances had been trying to get him to tackle ever since I had moved in. This was the writing of a booklet about the lives of several dozen famous and unknown magicians that was needed to accompany a set of slides of magic posters which Magic, Inc. was selling. I volunteered to undertake this project and it carried me through my remaining months with the Marshalls. It also brought my name back to mind. Frances once again began calling me David or, as in years past, "my boy."

When I finally left Magic, Inc., it was without goodbyes. I felt, for many years afterward, "part of the family." It was a privilege walking into the magic shop, maneuvering through a crowd of customers, and entering the back of the shop where Frances and her helpers greeted me and asked me how I was doing. I bought a building of my own in a suburb of Chicago called Glenwood; I lived upstairs and used the downstairs for my start-up book publishing business. Frances frequently offered me suggestions on how to keep my business flourishing. "Don't let a book go out of print," she advised.

She had been a willing but unsuccessful matchmaker for me while I lived with them. She once had me escort a Marshall family relative to a magic function, which kept a frozen frown on Jay's face until the evening was over. As I entered middle age as a bachelor Frances often reminded me it was time to get married. Once, wanting me to come to a gathering at their little theater, Jay reported that Frances had said, "Invite that Lonesome Glenwood." When I did marry she was sure to invite both my wife and me to their Christmas, birthday and anniversary parties. She was also sure to ask us if any "important announcement" was forthcoming. Our experience must certainly have been shared by others, for Frances was interested in many people's lives and welfare, even into future generations.

The breakneck routine which she carried on in the magic shop could not last forever, and she finally gave up many of her duties. In later years she was in and out of the hospital. Once when I called to wish her well, she said, "You should get younger friends." Perhaps I could, but there were no replacements for Frances and Jay.

Soon after one of those hospital stays, I made a date to have dinner with the Marshalls in a neighborhood restaurant. They were waiting for me in the magic shop when I arrived. As we stood talking, a father and his son came into the shop. The boy was slight and frail and no more than twelve years old. Neatly dressed in a suit and tie, he looked as if he had stepped out of the past. But like all boys in a magic shop, his eyes were bright and curious, and he was willing to see every trick in the shop demonstrated before spending his money. When he bought his trick it was clear he was unwilling to go, and watching him brought tears to the eyes of the three of us. Frances and Jay must have been reminded of the countless boys who had come and gone in their magic shop. I was reminded of the boy I had been forty years before.

Credits

The conjuror on the title page is shown performing the Cups and Balls, believed to be the oldest trick in magic. His table-top, supported by a writer's quill pen and a lithographer's grease pencil, represents a bound volume of the 19th-century periodical *Le Journal Amusant*. The artist, Alfred Grévin (1827–1892), was an illustrator for this journal and the *Petit Journal Pour Rire*. The drawing of the conjuror was a gift from Alexander Adrion, and Bob Read provided information about the artist.

The epigraph on page vii is taken from the poem "Elegy" by Jean Parrish.

Portions of the text previously appeared in different form in the following publications or were presented as papers at meetings.

A portion of the introduction appeared as *A Collector's Tale*, No. 3 of a series of chapbooks published by the Sun Dog Press. Copyright © 1995 by the Sun Dog Press.

"Regretting and Getting" was first published in *Collectors' Forum*.

"Houdini—Lost and Found," "A Glimpse of Martin Sunshine," "Generation Lux," "Portrait of a Popularizer" and "Fran and Me" appeared originally in *The Linking Ring*, the journal of the International Brotherhood of Magicians.

"My 'Discoverie' of Witchcraft" was published in *Biblio: The Magazine for Books, Magazines and Ephemera*.

"Portrait of a Popularizer" was initially a presentation at the 6th Los Angeles Conference on Magic History. Photographs, ephemera and correspondence of Barrows Mussey are published through the courtesy of Mrs. Dagmar Mussey. Thanks to Richard Hatch for helpful information and to Matthew Ainsworth for researching publishing records in New York City.

"Dealing with Dr. Hall" was a presentation given at the 24th Annual Magic Collectors' Weekend. The portrait of Dr. Hall appeared in *Old Conjuring Books,* published by Gerald Duckworth & Company Limited, London, in 1972, and is reprinted with permission. Selections of correspondence from Dr. Trevor H. Hall are printed through the courtesy of Mrs. Marguerite Hall.

"Postscript to the Hall Affair" first appeared as "Stumbling Into Scholarship" in *Magicol,* a journal of the Magic Collectors' Association.

"Fran and Me" was published as a limited-edition keepsake accompanying the panel discussion "Stage Magicians and Magic Books in Chicago: Some History and Reminiscences," presented at the 18th Annual Printers Row Book Fair.

Index

INCLINED TOWARD MAGIC

was designed by Daniel Franklin and composed by Village Typographers, Inc. of Belleville, Illinois, in the typeface Requiem.

Jonathan Hoefler based his design of Requiem on a set of inscriptional capitals appearing in Ludovico Vicentino degli Arrighi's 1523 writing manual *Il Modo de Temperare le Penne.*